LIBRARY SERVICES

TO THE

DISADVANTAGED

LIBRARY SERVICES

TO THE

DISADVANTAGED

edited by

WILLIAM MARTIN

LINNET BOOKS & CLIVE BINGLEY

FIRST PUBLISHED 1975 BY CLIVE BINGLEY LTD
16 PEMBRIDGE ROAD LONDON W11
SIMULTANEOUSLY PUBLISHED IN THE USA BY LINNET BOOKS
AN IMPRINT OF THE SHOE STRING PRESS INC
995 SHERMAN AVENUE HAMDEN CONNECTICUT 06514
SET IN 10 ON 12 POINT PRESS ROMAN
BY CREATIVE OFFSET LTD KINGSTON UPON THAMES
PRINTED AND BOUND IN GREAT BRITAIN BY
REDWOOD BURN LTD TROWBRIDGE AND ESHER
COPYRIGHT © WILLIAM MARTIN 1975
ALL RIGHTS RESERVED
BINGLEY ISBN: 0 8157 203 0
LINNET ISBN: 0-208-01372-5

Library of Congress Cataloging in Publication Data
Main entry under title:

Library services to the disadvantaged.

    Includes bibliographical references.
    1. Libraries and the socially handicapped--Addresses,
essays, lectures. 2. Libraries and community--Addresses,
essays, lectures. 3. Libraries and foreign population--
Addresses, essays, lectures. 4. Prison libraries--
Addresses, essays, lectures. I. Martin, William J.
Z711.92.S6L53 1975   027.6   75-12955
ISBN 0-208-01372-5

CONTENTS

TO THE PEOPLE OF WEST BELFAST

This collection of papers is an attempt to bring together in convenient form the diverse views and experiences of several groups and professions with an interest in the role of the library in society. The contributors, who include librarians, social workers and academics in various parts of the world, are firm believers in the need for a much more positive commitment by public libraries to the development of the communities of which they are a part, and particularly to the needs of disadvantaged people within these communities. As with all such works, many debts were incurred in its making, and these I now gratefully acknowledge. Thanks are due to my contributors to whom the boundaries of time, distance and language eventually proved no obstacle, and to the College of Librarianship Wales for permission to include a section from Susan Croker's project on immigrants, number 5 in their *Student series*. A great deal is also owed to Dr Ken Brown of the Department of Social and Economic History, Queens University, to my long-suffering Head of Department Arthur Maltby, and to my family.

William J Martin
Belfast, The Queens University. January 1975.

INTRODUCTION

W J MARTIN

A noticeable feature of the activities of librarians in recent years has been a growing interest in the role of the library in society. One aspect of this overall development has been a closer involvement of librarians with the problems of service to the disadvantaged. This book originated with the realisation that not only were such developments underway, but also that the challenge of serving the disadvantaged is now being taken up all over the world. Hence, it was felt that by bringing together an international collection of responses to specific situations some light might be shed on common problems.

Given the nature of the library reply to these problems, it is difficult to avoid the conclusion that the time of the disadvantaged is now upon us. It is true that throughout history librarians have been conscious of their social role, but the response of the library profession to the social problems of the 1960s and 1970s has been such as to herald a qualitative change in professional attitudes and actions. Like all change this has not gone unchallenged, and many librarians have reacted strongly against what they perceive to be an unwarranted switch in professional direction. However, what has occurred has not been so much a change of direction as a change in emphasis following on a reappraisal of traditional library aims and practices, and their restatement in the changed circumstances of the last quarter of the twentieth century. Raised on ideals of service to the community, librarians engaged in work with the disadvantaged are simply living up to these ideals by reacting in appropriate ways to social concerns.(1)

Central to the entire debate is the question of whether or not social concerns are appropriately those of librarians. The contributors to this volume are in no doubt on this point and, indeed, the social commitment which has brought them together is a keynote of the work. However, the very concept of service to the disadvantaged is in itself testimony to the many divergent interpretations of the nature of library service. There can be few definitions which do not admit of more than one interpretation. Moreover, while all must be taken in context it should be remembered that this context is seldom static but more usually in process of change. Small wonder then that librarians can hold differing views of their professional 'raison d'etre', when the same mix of factors which can constitute a successful library service in one context may be seen as ineffective, even irrelevant, in another. By way of example let us consider two definitions of library service:- ' The facilities provided by a library for the use of books and the dissemination of information.'(2) 'Activities or programmes undertaken in addition to or in place of ordinary library services, with the intention of reaching a disadvantaged population.'(3)

The first of these quotations clearly refers to the traditional idea of a library service, and as such it is a perfectly adequate definition. It would on the other hand, be of little use to anyone interested in library service to the disadvantaged because, as the second example shows, this involves rather more than the simple extension of everyday library service to disadvantaged groups, implying as it does recognition of the special needs of such people. Furthermore, the second definition accords with the need to reach out and serve people where it will do the most good, in their own communities. This brings us to another keynote of this present volume, an adherence to the concept of 'outreach' or, 'The extension of public library services beyond traditional patterns.'(4)

Now although the outreach approach is characteristic of work with the disadvantaged, it is also to be found in more orthodox library settings, for imaginative librarians will reach out to their publics wherever the occasion permits. One makes this point in order to dispel any notions of superiority, or indeed of schism, for there is no 'right' or 'wrong' way in this, but rather the 'library way'. This is so, whether one is talking about a suburban branch or an inner city storefront library: at all times the public should be the main focus of attention. Hence, there is a certain plausibility in the argument that would deny both the existence of, and the need for, any such phenomenon as library service to the disadvantaged, for after all, library service is library service, period. There is, however, a flaw in this argument, and it lies in the implied assumption that library service is everywhere of a universally adequate standard, and that all sections of the public are thus served. Such is scarcely the case, as is all too evident from the statistics for use, and non-use, of public libraries. Furthermore, as library services have developed, discrete groups of readers have emerged as targets for specifically orientated library service of a type suited to their requirements as a group. Children and young people have long been one example of such a group, the disadvantaged are now emerging as another. In singling out the disadvantaged as subjects for special treatment, librarians are simply recognising the advantages of delineating a particular area of activity with its own parameters, resource allocations and methods of work.

In taking such action not only are librarians operating in a long tradition of social involvement, (5) but also they are working in their own best interests. Only by such conscious efforts can the profession hope to narrow the 'performance gap' between library potential and library use. As the disadvantaged are not by any means prominent on library membership roles, even moderately successful efforts to entice them into the library have been hailed as minor triumphs, particularly so where these have involved services to adults. Moreover, in reaching out to the disadvantaged, libraries are operating in an area of activity already occupied by other public service departments, especially in the fields of health, education and welfare, where strenuous efforts are being made to provide community services at a level, and in a form, commensurate with community demands. Arguably, however, the major breakthrough in library circles has been the newly awakened social consciousness of recent years. For many librarians today, the old passive role of libraries as a minority service, existing merely to serve the reading and information needs of society is no longer acceptable. Socially-conscious librarians seek to serve all the public, not just a minority, and they view the library as being one of several institutions working within society whose overall aim is the improvement of social conditions and the development of human resources. To this end they seek to act, as librarians, by bringing their library skills and training to bear where they will have most effect. This implies neither abdication of responsibility for existing library users, nor the arrogation of duties more properly the concern of others, but is rather, recognition of the library's proper place in the overall scheme of community service.

It is certainly the library's place to provide the public with the full range of library services, print and non-print. What is equally certain, if rather less obvious, is the duty of librarians to add their expertise to the struggle against those social evils which beset society, the evils of poverty, discrimination, inequality and crime. Not that librarians have the answer to all, or even any, of these problems. Rather it is likely that the ultimate solution will reside within society as a whole, in future cooperation between the social services, including the library service. Nevertheless, if one accepts that librarians have not only the opportunity but also the ability, to liase between the casualties of society and any likely sources of aid then, almost as a corollary, one must accept that they have a duty to do so. They must go into their own communities and seek out the social problems of the day. They must identify the people suffering from the effects of these problems, and endeavour to bring them into contact with total community resources via the resources of the library. Even this fundamental step, the matter of gaining the attention of disadvantaged people, will prove to be sufficient of a challenge. Herein lies the rationale for library service to the disadvantaged, and it is based on a paradox. In all modern societies there are to be found groups of disadvantaged people: people in need of assistance, people in need of information, or in other words, people in need of a decent library service. Above all, however, is the fact that for most of these people, the existence of the library is a matter of supreme indifference.

Before focussing on the groups and individuals concerned, one must first discuss the problems of definition raised by use of the term 'disadvantaged'. It is not proposed to re-open here the terminological discussion on the differences between, say, 'disadvantaged' and 'deprived'. For present purposes, they will both be taken as indications of the existence of want or of needs waiting to be served. On this point the reader is referred to Eleanor F Brown *Library service to the disadvantaged* Methuen, New Jersey, Scarecrow Press, 1971. 'The disadvantaged' is one of those terms that have developed as a result of everyday use rather than as the outcome of deliberate or scientific thought. Like all such terms it is far from perfect, and while its apparent neutrality and essential vagueness have probably encouraged its use, (6) there are, nonetheless, distinct problems attendant upon this use. In the first place, 'disadvantaged' is a relative concept, the employment of which implies the presence of certain criteria, themselves usually the product of a particular type of society. Secondly, whatever the criteria involved, or the social organisation concerned, the influence of value judgements can never be completely discounted.

On the first point, let us consider the poor peasant, newly arrived as an immigrant in some western industrial centre. Disadvantaged he may be in comparison to his indigenous workmates, but he is likely to be much better off, at least in material terms, than the majority of his fellows back in the homeland. Another aspect of disadvantage is that which obtains where disparities in living standards exist between various groups indigenous to a particular country, for instance the offspring of immigrant parents and those born of native stock. This is the principle of 'relative deprivation' so admirably described by the American Michael Harrington, who found that black Americans, with a living standard the envy of most of the people of the world, still felt deprived in relation to the higher levels of consumption being enjoyed by white Americans.(7)

With regard to the second point, whereas the condition of disadvantage is an observable fact, the mere designation of people as 'disadvantaged' in itself may be said to represent the application of value judgements. Furthermore, does not the opposition of the people so designated indicate the presence of other value judgements, marking a reaction against further stigmatisation by society? Unfortunately, the term 'disadvantaged' still carries with it a suggestion of failure, of the opposite to 'advantaged' with all its overtones of social superiority, good taste, and the good life. Not even Websters Dictionary is entirely blameless in this respect for whereas its designation 'Lacking in the basic resource or conditions ... necessary for an equal position in society' (8) is relative, it also permits of a negative construction which emphasises peoples' shortcomings rather than the qualities that they may have to offer. There is no disputing the need for such criteria or for social norms against which the incidence of disadvantage may be measured; and facts are, after all, neutral. Nevertheless, one could wish for greater objectivity in the response from society to the conclusions drawn from such data. If disadvantaged people exist in all societies, it is what society chooses to do about them that causes the 'problem' of the disadvantaged.

Accordingly, the concept of disadvantage can be seen to comprise several elements:- An unfavourable position in society; a position of relative deprivation; minority group status consequent upon the relatively low regard in which the group is held; an inability to redress this situation without the cooperation of members of the majority; a lack of opportunity; opportunity to maximise individual potential and to gain entry into the socio-economic mainstream. This final element may be seen as both cause and effect in the plight of the disadvantaged because lack of opportunity, not innate inability or laziness or disinterest, is very often the final arbiter. In the Ballymurphy district of Belfast for example, when opportunity was seen to exist the true potential of the people was revealed. See 'Two outreach experiments in West Belfast' below.

Identification of the disadvantaged is made more difficult by an unhelpful tendency in the literature to lump together all those forms of library service where the patrons are in some way disadvantaged: the sick and the handicapped, the socially inadequate, and the members of various minority groups. The sick and the incapacitated, both mentally and physically, are without doubt disadvantaged, but the complex of library systems that has developed to serve them is much less evidence of sectional autonomy within the disadvantaged sector, than it is a response to a distinctly different kind of problem. This separate aspect of work with the disadvantaged is dealt with elsewhere and is, therefore, excluded from consideration in this volume.

A further obstacle to identification is the confusion which often results from the use of prefixes such as 'cultural', 'linguistic' or 'educational,' ironically with the purpose of clarifying the link between the several kinds of disadvantage and their cause. Although such nuances of disadvantage can be shown to exist, the effort required to do so can often be counterproductive in that, apart from a certain amount of definitional 'hair-splitting', the basic underlying fact of disadvantage is liable to be overlooked. Therefore, while such concepts as 'social' or 'cultural' or 'economic' disadvantage, to name but the main sub-classes, may be useful adjuncts to the study of the subject, the artificial character of all these distinctions should not be forgotten. What for example, is unemployment? Is it evidence of social or of economic disadvantage? Or, indeed, is it really a cultural problem? The point of course is that disadvantage is frequently a cumulative affair, where particular groups of people fall prey to several handicaps at the same time, and different groupings exhibit similar symptoms of disadvantage. People in prison and poor immigrant workers may both share the fact of their illiteracy, just as those in poor circumstances can be impecunious, badly-educated, and unemployed all at the same time. Furthermore, just as these people have a cumulative aspect, so they are also to be found in a localised form. Thus can a British government circular speak of '...multiple deprivation arising from overcrowding of homes, family sizes much above the average, high incidence of supplements in cash or in kind from the state, high incidence of truancy or poor attendance, a rapid turnover of teachers or difficulty in attracting them to the district; and the general quality of the physical environment.'(9)

In Britain, recognition of this localised incidence of disadvantage has led to official intervention, with certain parts of the country being designated as 'Educational Priority Areas' and others as 'Areas of Social Need'. (10) In many countries, moreover, librarians have been active in such areas of social distress and in a great many cases this represents a conscious effort to play a more dynamic role in the social process: to help initiate social change instead of simply following in its wake. Something of the work of these librarians is described in the following chapters, and in the main these comprise efforts to help specific groups of people, the victims of particular social problems, the problems resulting from poverty, immigration, illiteracy and imprisonment. Apart from the common burden of disadvantage, which all of them share, these groups may be identified by socio-economic criteria, by levels of income, standards of housing, occupational status, and similar relatively objective criteria. Therefore, they serve both to emphasise the socio-economic theme of the book, and to meet any charges of bias through the use of 'culturally-loaded' terminology. It has been found that phrases using the word 'cultural' are often means of belittling the culture of minority ethnic groups.

That such groupings exist in many countries is one thing; that their existence can be recorded in precise definitional form is something else again. Who, for instance, are the 'poor'? What is meant by the term 'poverty'? There is certainly an income element to all of this, in that an individual or a family can be in the position where income is insufficient to meet basic minimum needs. However,

13

it is now recognised, particularly in modern consumer-type economies, that any definition of poverty must allow for provision of the 'conventional necessities', which today would include items of entertainment or recreation.(11) Indeed, in many Western countries the share of personal incomes allocated to the satisfaction of basic needs is steadily in decline. (12) Furthermore, poverty can never be an entirely objective concept, and every poverty definition must allow for some element of 'felt needs', for it is always possible to feel poor regardless of the level of one's income.(13) Above all, poverty is a relative concept, meaningful only in the context of the society where the definition is to be applied. Therefore, as it is presently interpreted, poverty exists where one's personal circumstances are at variance with the accepted norms of society, norms of consumption, expectation and self-respect.(14) The problem in defining poverty is, in fact, largely a cultural problem, as it involves making decisions about what people require in order to be able to function adequately in society. (15)

In order to measure poverty and to determine the extent of this inadequate social functioning, governments have from time to time, employed various objective criteria. Two broad classes of criteria are in general use: the absolute and the relative. As one recent authority explains, 'The former involves assigning a price tag to the necessities of life (the 'poverty line') and designating as poor those whose income falls below that figure. When the latter standard is used, the bottom segment of the income distribution is the poverty group.'(16)

Normally based on a calculation of the minimum income necessary to provide the basic nutritional needs, the 'poverty line' has ranged from the United States version with its 'minimum sufficient to maintain a hypothetical family of four',(17) to the British equivalent, based variously on the average industrial wage (18) and the scale of minimum living requirements laid down by the Supplementary Benefits Commission.(19) According to this scale, benefits are paid depending on the amount by which a person's requirements exceed his resources. Thus, a person whose income from all sources is less than he would receive in supplementary benefits can be said to be living in official poverty.

The many difficulties inherent in the use of absolute standards of poverty, and in particular the essential relativity of all such absolutes, has prompted the application of relative standards of poverty. These relative standards are reflected in the sets of indices which have been designed to assist in the quantification of poverty, indices embracing not only personal data such as calorie intake, life expectancy and the like, but also data relating to society as a whole, for instance, the extent of urbanisation.(20) Even relative standards pose problems, however, because the decision as to who will comprise the bottom segment of society is itself related to some absolute notion of an adequate minimum.(21) In neither case, moreover, are the decisions taken in a political vacuum because the official recognition of poverty, and any subsequent attempts at its elimination, of necessity involve the electorate, which untimately has to pay for such programmes.(22)

Whatever the method of measurement, and bearing in mind the dangers of international comparisons, there can be few developed societies today which are completely free of poverty, and in fact, many possess substantial pockets of it. (23) As a rule, the 'poverty profile' shows great similarities between one western country and another, with essentially the same groups of people coming at the bottom of the pile in most places. The main groups living in poverty or with the greatest chance of being poor, are the old, the sick and the chronically handicapped, the unemployed, the low paid, and families where the children are entirely supported by the mother. Finally, mention should be made of those people who, while not literally living in poverty, could nevertheless be said to suffer from the 'poverty of opportunity', In this category one would include the residents of redevelopment areas, of 'difficult' housing estates, and ethnic or religious ghettoes, all places where the physical or social environment has an adverse effect on the quality of life. Although this may take one onto the thin ice of value judgement, many modern poverty thinkers would include consideration of this environmental deprivation.

The problems of poverty appear at many points in the collection of papers that follow, and, indeed, if there is such a thing as a 'common denominator of disadvantage' then this could well be it. Poverty is an identifiable theme in no less than six of the sections: John Colson's historical survey of work with the disadvantaged in the United States, Jenny Armour's chapter on outreach in the London Borough of Lambeth, Gerry Finnegan's guide to community contact for librarians, Marie - Anne Hulshoff's report on social work within a Dutch library system, my own section on West Belfast, and Ken Gilmore's final comparative chapter. Its

15

presence is implicit in the background of the remaining chapters.

Poverty and its effects are no strangers to another of the groups of people featured in this book, the immigrants. Not that all immigrants are poor, or even disadvantaged, however, although large numbers of them could be so described. The fact is that migration is another one of those subjects the study of which is bedevilled by intolerance, a lack of objectivity, and the absence of reliable statistical data. It is, moreover an international phenomenon, (24) which means that when difficulties over some aspect of migration arise, they can occasionally attain international proportions. Prominent in any list of these difficulties would be that of definition, of finding general agreement upon terminology. The term 'migration' is generally taken to refer to the geographical movement of either individuals or groups, although this simplest of definitions conceals a complex of such movements both within and across international borders.(25) Although man continues to exhibit his traditional propensity to migrate, recent decades have seen some notable changes in the character of this migration. Thus, while the volume of migration across oceans has decreased considerably, international migration within politically-divided continents has maintained its intensity, subject always to certain measures of control.(26) The motives for migration remain as diverse as ever, although internal migration for the purpose of land settlement is now confined to one or two countries.(27) Refugees continue to comprise a rather special type of migrant in that the decision to migrate is taken under duress.(28) Such people may be described as 'involuntary migrants' in contrast to, say, that great majority of immigrants to Western Europe since 1945 who, moving for largely economic reasons, may be described as 'voluntary migrants'.(29) Unquestionably, no matter how diverse the circumstances, in virtually every country in the world, there has occurred a movement from the land to the cities, internal migration from areas of low economic growth into areas of high economic growth. (30) Such internal migrations while bringing their own special difficulties in the shape of pressure upon the public services, on living space and other resources, are nevertheless, usually spared the worst excesses of the international migratory experience. Therefore, while people from outside a particular region may be viewed with suspicion, their presence is unlikely to cause the same kind of alarm which, in some circles, greets the arrival of immigrants

16

from another country. Indeed, if these newcomers happen to be people of a different race the outcome is not infrequently a problem of race relations. Hence, in countries such as Britain, the race relations approach has tended to dominate research into immigration, which is hardly surprising when one considers that in Britain, the term 'immigrant' has become virtually synonymous with 'black man'.(31)

As for 'immigration' here also is a term which is capable of varying interpretations. In Britain, particularly, difficulties have arisen, especially the occasionally quite confusing approaches of the various government departments to this question. Some authorities would distinguish between 'permanent migration' where the immigrant has moved from one country to another for a period of at least one year, and 'temporary migration', where the stay has been for more than one month but less than a year.(32) Others would apply the term in a broader sense arguing that no rigid distinction is possible between permanent and temporary migration, and pointing out that while most individual immigrants come for a limited period only, immigrants as a group are permanently present.(33) Therefore, any definition of immigrants would include temporary or seasonal migrants as well as permanent migrants to a country, and of course, their dependants.

In general, it is the immigration aspect of the question which is the most acute source of difficulty, as people in the host countries react in various ways against the influx of immigrants from different national, racial and cultural backgrounds. Despite the myriad circumstances of individual immigrants, however, there are strong similarities in the experiences of all immigrant groups. In addition to the common motive for immigration, the economic motive, there are the shared experiences resulting from prejudice and discrimination, especially in the fields of housing, employment and education. Clearly, as a result of geographical, historical, social and political factors there are also differences in the collective experiences of immigrants, most plausibly in the case of migrations to the countries of the old world and to those of the new. European immigrants to Australia, for example, are unlikely to suffer quite the same level of indignity imposed upon those residents of the former overseas colonies come to work in the industrial centres of Europe. Whereas it is possible to argue that this is at bottom a question of class, thus casting doubts on the race relations approach,(34) it is also arguable that the worst instances of native reaction have tended to polarize around the factor of race. In Britain, for example, the strongest reaction has been reserved, not for the Irish who comprise by far the largest single immigrant group, but for immigrants from the New Commonwealth who, although numerically much less significant, are overwhelmingly coloured.

One result has been the exclusion of British passport holders from the UK while foreigners, that is citizens of the Irish Republic, have been free to come and go. Such developments notwithstanding, all immigrants are placed under stress of one kind or another, if only the kind of stress which results from being 'different'. Such pressure may of course lead to various forms of mental illness, and to the condition of 'marginality' whereby a person can find himself in a kind of psychological no-man's land between two cultures.

As these pressures begin to work, the immigrant may strive for a measure of acceptance in the new society. This striving may take the form of an adjustment of immigrant habits to the extent necessary for survival in the new environment, to a search for 'accommodation'.(35) The process can, however, go through several stages of development depending upon the immigrant group concerned and, of course, upon the attitudes of the host society. It can, for instance, go so far as 'assimilation', where the group may adjust itself so completely to its new surroundings that it merges into the host society and loses its separate identity.(36) Or it can reach the stage of 'integration', a term which in its current interpretation refers to a situation where the immigrant group while retaining its own culture and religion, becomes adapted to, and is accepted as, a permanent part of the host society.(37) As Nicholas Deakin points out, 'This form of integration ----- in the sense of a part being integrated into the whole while retaining its separate identity ----- is sometimes called cultural pluralism ... and ... it involves the coexistence and mutual tolerance of several cultures within one society.'(38)

This latter stage of affairs is generally regarded as desirable in liberal circles although, more often than not, it remains an ideal, a far-off objective, with the reality often comprising a grudging accommodation between immigrant groups and the indigenous population. Sue Croker's work on Asian immigrants in Britain broadly confirms this sombre if more realistic description of immigrant-native relations.

The problems resulting from illiteracy can truly be said to be worldwide, both in their distribution and in their effects. Until comparatively recently this was seen as a problem for the developing nations, of interest to the west, but only on academic or humanitarian grounds. Recent studies have changed all this, and although illiteracy is still mainly prevalent in countries of Asia, Africa and Latin America, it exists to an alarming extent in several of the most highly developed societies of the west. In England and Wales, for instance, recent and widely-accepted figures would indicate that some 2 million people, or about 6% of the adult population, are functionally illiterate.(39) Moreover, the results of a Harris Poll held in the United States during 1970, indicate a figure of some 18.5 million Americans who are, likewise, functional illiterates.(40)

As will be apparent from the use of the prefix, one is concerned here with two aspects of illiteracy, the traditional mass illiteracy that is indeed prevalent in many countries of the third world, and the more recently acknowledged functional illiteracy, which occurs within the developed nations of the world. One would emphasise, nonetheless, that while the character and location of these respective literacy problems may differ, one is dealing with basically the same kind of problem, the problem of illiteracy. Therefore, as regards the incidence of disadvantage, who would be likely to be the worse off, the total illiterate living in a largely illiterate country, or the functional illiterate in a country with a high level of literacy? The answer is that levels of literacy are relative and have to be judged in the context of the society concerned. Therefore, the basic level of literacy necessary for any society would be such as would allow people to function adequately within that society. To this extent, therefore, there is no difference in the essential purpose of the various literacy campaigns, which would appear to be the dissemination of fundamental skills in reading and writing. Hence, functional literacy is the goal, not just in the western countries but in the third world as well, where its attainment is viewed as being of cardinal importance to the development process.(41)

Moreover, when one examines the terminology, one is struck by the similarities that obtain between the definitions concerned. Thus, literacy is defined as, 'The degree of dissemination among a

country's population of the dual skills of reading and writing ...'
(42) This makes no mention of the level of skill required and,
indeed, if one quotes further, the affinity to functional literacy
becomes very strong. 'Here a literate society is one in which most
adult members can read and write at least a simple message,(43)
Functional literacy has in its turn been defined as follows. 'A
person is functionally literate when he has command of reading
skills that permit him to go about his daily activities successfully
on the job, or to move about society normally with comprehension
of the usual printed expressions and messages he encounters.' (44)
Arguably, if present efforts to achieve widespread functional
literacy were to succeed then there would be no literacy problem
as such, because the target groups would then be capable of
playing an adequate social and occupational role.

Nevertheless, such is the extent of mass illiteracy in the world,
and so widespread are its ramifications, that the attainment of
such ends is going to take a very long time. In western Europe, for
example, the process of transition from a position of general
illiteracy to one of moderate levels of literacy took from 75 to 100
years.(45) In Japan, usually regarded as an outstanding example,
it took 'some 50 years of exceptional and constant effort'.(46)
Nor is effort in itself likely to prove any guarantee of success
because this is not simply a question of the widespread diffusion
of education, but involves, '...complex multidimensional
phenomena that can be explained only by a series of factors:
historical, geographical, economical, political, cultural, sociological
and psychological...'(47)

The west, with its early start in the race for industrialization,
has a disproportionate share of the world's literate population, in
the same way that it has a disproportionate share of world gross
national product and industrial power. That this should be so is
no mere accident because it reflects the strong correlation between
industrialization and GNP on the one hand, and literacy on the
other. Japan will again serve as a useful example because, whereas
it has only some 6% to 7% of the population of Asia, it has at
least 20% of its adult literates. It is also one of the world's great
industrial powers.

The global figures on the other hand are hardly encouraging,
with something of the order of 800 million adult illiterates present
in the world today. (49) Admittedly, this figure represents a fall in

the world illiteracy rate from a level of 39.3% in 1960 to one of 34.2% in 1970, with a further fall expected to 29% by 1980.(50) These figures, however, are for total illiterates, for people who can neither read or write. They exclude from consideration all those people who have some reading ability but not enough to put to any real practical use, the functional illiterates.

Therefore, the struggle against illiteracy is a difficult one because illiteracy, in its various guises, is one of the world's major social diseases. In the third world it helps to prolong exploitation and thus leads to untold misery, social and political instability, and the hindrance of economic growth. In industrial societies too, the impact of illiteracy may be detected in all the indices of human suffering from the welfare rolls to prison populations. One state in America recently estimated that 55% of its prison inmates were illiterates.(51) This is a problem, therefore, that entails costs for the whole of society as well as for those who suffer most immediately from its consequences. Nor, indeed, have the efforts against the problem been conspicuously successful, not even where national governments have thrown their weight behind such campaigns. Estimates for the United States indicate that, at best, the government funded adult basic education programmes have reached only about 3% of the illiterate adult population.(52) This postulates the need for community involvement with the problem and hence, for the intervention of librarians. Margaret Redfern deals at length with the problems of illiteracy in Britain, and her chapter indicates several ways in which this intervention may be attempted.

There can be few countries in the world today that are free of the problems of crime and, indeed, if the mass media are any guide, mankind is becoming rapidly more lawless. Therefore, for the last of the disadvantaged groups covered in this book, one has chosen a single element from the complex of interrelationships that is crime and punishment, the inmates of prisons and other penal institutions. Some may question the validity of including prisoners in any consideration of the disadvantaged, but the fact is that they are at a disadvantage, both in the closed world of prison, and in that greater society of which they have fallen foul.

As for their actions, although deemed anti- social, crime is not something that is inherently alien to society but, in fact, is something that occurs within society and is part of the structure of society.(53) Indeed, one can go beyond this to assert that in laying down its norms of social behaviour, society not only creates crime, but also criminals, as criminal status is something that is ascribed.(54) Furthermore, the likelihood of these people continuing with a career of crime is greatly increased by the official punishment process, which not only stamps them as criminal but can also offer them a passport to the sub-culture of the criminal underworld.(55)

There is no lack of statistical data on the incidence of crime in all its aspects, although one must be careful to distinguish between what these figures purport to represent and what they in fact show.(56) In England and Wales, the number of indictable offences known to the police has risen from an annual average of around 500,000 in the 1950's to more than 1 million a year since 1965.(57) In the United States, Federal Bureau of Investigation 'index crimes' reported to the police remained at a rate of around 1% of the population during the 1950's, but doubled during the 1960's from 2 million to 4 million.(58) In Japan, on the other hand, adult crime levels have fallen steadily since the mid-1950's, accompanied however, by a sharp increase in minor violations.(59) In some countries, moreover, serious crimes are increasingly being committed by young people, and this is true of both the developed and developing nations. In England and Wales, for example, two-thirds of the convictions for indictable offences are of persons under the age of 25,(60) while in Hong Kong, the under-25's comprise about half the persons convicted of serious and violent crimes.(61)

As a method of social defence against crime, most societies have resorted to the process of imprisoning offenders, frequently under isolated and punitive conditions. However, the punitive approach has been heavily criticised for both its ineffectiveness and its cost,(62) and indeed, any modern attempt at costing would include a consideration of the social cost involved in terms of lives wasted behind bars. To an unprecedented extent, society now recognises some measure of responsibility for the fate of the offender. At one level, this assumption of responsibility can materialize through the incorporation of social defence consider-ations into plans for social and economic development, in order to neutralize any possible side effects.(63) At another it can be manifest in the provision of programmes aimed at the rehabilitation of individual offenders.

Imprisonment still remains society's principal answer to the criminal tendencies of its weaker brethren, particularly for adult offenders. It is likely to remain so for the forseeable future. However, within the scope of the prison system many important modifications have already made their appearance, not least in the fields of education, labour and prison administration. Elementary education is now viewed as being of the foremost importance in the social readjustment of offenders, and most countries now have some form of educational facility in their prisons. Aimed increasingly at imparting a basic social education, these facilities can range from classes at which attendance is compulsory, (Chile, rather surprisingly, has reported the presence of compulsory schooling in all its prisons) to the kind of voluntary classes held at British prisons. Obviously, what are reported as 'educational facilities' can at times comprise the most rudimentary of provision, in the same way as pathetic little collections of books can be glorified with the name of 'library'.

As for prison labour, this too is increasingly being viewed in the light of the prisoner's future needs, and experiments have taken place both with incentive schemes and with vocationally orientated work. In this latter context, advances have been made through the introduction of occupations closely related to the background and potentialities of the prisoners. This has been of great significance in the training of agricultural labour, although technical training opportunities are also available in some places, notably it seems in Israel where, '...training is given in carpentry, auto-mechanics, plumbing, tailoring, hair cutting, shoemaking, laundering, assembling of electrical appliances and fittings, toy manufacturing, and vegetable and flower gardening.'(64)

In some countries, in an attempt to counteract the negative influence of prison, and to strengthen the individual's sense of social responsibility, schemes have been introduced to enable prisoners to participate in selected aspects of the administration of the institution. This process has been particularly well-developed in Finland where, in all institutions, trusted prisoners may acquire the status of limited self-government.(65) This trend towards a democratisation of the penal system can be casually linked to certain fundamental aspects of the western social structure, including a movement for lay control of many areas of

23

activity where the 'experts' have been found wanting.(66) Conceivably this could eventually lead to inmate participation at all levels in the operation of the prison system, but the available evidence would appear to support very little in the way of such radical departures. Thus, while the European Committee Study did find certain traces of this democratic decision - making process, these were few, and confined to minor issues, with the major aspects of institutional control still firmly in the hands of the authorities.(67) In any case, even allowing for some likely development in this direction, it is debatable whether this 'democratisation' constitutes anything more than 'reformist tinkering' with the established penal system, a development which in the long-run could well prove to be anti-progressive.(68) Arguably, a more fruitful approach would lie in the introduction of better after-care and release programmes, an increased use of the open prison idea, and a wider recourse to probation as an alternative to prison. For instance, the ratio of offenders on probation, that is, undergoing non-institutional curtailment of freedom, to prisoners sentenced to institutional deprivation of freedom, can range from four to one in the United Kingdom and the Netherlands, as against one to two in France.(69) While according to similar international estimates, one out of every three prisoners may be found suitable for open institutions.(70) Of course for many reformers, the ultimate aim is the complete abolition of the prison system. As will be clear from his contribution, on the Hall and Haga Prisons in Sweden, Lennart Enge belongs to this latter school of thought. His chapter is of particular interest, therefore, in that it portrays the work of a radical librarian in a reasonably advanced prison system. Gordon Kirby's study on the other hand, will make much more familiar reading, for although it deals with prison library services in Australia, the work that it describes is much more in the mainstream of traditional prison librarianship.

It is to be hoped that the collection as a whole will facilitate other such comparisons, and that the combination of broad survey - type articles with specific descriptions of individual projects will go some way towards meeting the needs both of the 'academic' reader and of the practising librarian with a specific problem in mind. Such works are by nature selective and the present volume is no exception. Thus, while aiming to bring some international perspective to what is now a common set of library problems, it leaves out a great deal not only in the way of individual projects, but also in terms of potential service groups. No mention will be found, therefore, of services to womens' groups, claimants unions, itinerants or gay people, not because these are deemed beyond the pale of disadvantage, but simply because they constitute largely 'unexplored areas' on the broad map of library provision.(71) However, the fact that such groupings have already begun to provide their own information services should be a matter of concern to all librarians. It could mean either that they have been denied service at the public library, or that the level of provision offered them did not meet their needs. It could also mean that they just do not consider the public library to be a likely source of supply for their information needs.

Always allowing for differences in timing, as well as in the character of the response, the reasons behind the quickening interest in the needs of the disadvantaged will be found, in most countries, to have been very similar. In almost every case a combination of 'push' factors and 'pull' factors will have been involved. As examples of the former, one would cite the continued minority status of the public library service in many countries, and the change that has overtaken the basic function of the public library. The maturing of general library facilities in certain countries, and the subsequent search for new areas of endeavour, as well as the prospect of increased leisure time for an increasingly better-educated population are examples of the latter.

It is difficult to ignore the consensus argument that in most countries with well-developed public library systems, the majority of the public remain largely indifferent to the presence of the library. In Britain, preliminary reports from the very recent survey of library provision in the London Borough of Hillingdon confirm many of the findings of earlier surveys. In particular, the indication is that some 70% of the population does not use the public library. Indeed, in the United States during the years from 1965 to 1968, public library circulation in places with populations of over 100,000 fell by 16%.(72) At about the same time there developed a series of outreach experiments, the forerunners of many user-orientated projects.(73) The contradiction between the theoretical definition of the library's public as the entire spectrum of the community, and the reality of its actual composition, was beginning to impinge upon the actions as well as the words of librarians. This in itself represented a recognition of the changing function of libraries, resulting from the influence of such external factors as the mass media, the paperback book, bookshops and educational technology.(74) There was also a certain amount of response to charges that the public libraries were irrelevant, inflexible, and incapable of real communication with ordinary people.

As an approach to such problems the concept of outreach has a good deal to offer. By definition outreach is flexible, as it involves the direction of specifically planned services at particular groups of users.(75) Furthermore, if these services were planned in consultation with the community and in accordance with its expressed wishes and needs, it would be well nigh impossible for them to be irrelevant. Again, this type of face-to-face contact with the public, replacing the corporate image with the personal one, is likely to prove the best available prospect for genuine communication between libraries and their clientele. In fact, this kind of communication really only develops from a positive involvement by the library in the life of the local community. Gerry Finnegan has several observations to make on this in his chapter, in the course of which he examines some of the terminology involved, including the use of the word 'community'. Sufficient at this stage, therefore, to point out that community is yet another term which is capable of being used in a variety of ways. For example, '... to describe an area on the one hand, where all the inhabitants are able to have face-to-face contacts, or on the other hand, an area the size of a large city. For some, the boundaries of their area may reflect merely administrative convenience; for others they may represent strong feelings of common interest.'(76) Hence to the outreach librarian, the community in one place may be comprised of an enclave of deprived families in some urban council estate, and in another, be composed of the inmates of the local prison. Whatever the case, the level of service, its materials, programmes, publicity, and personnel, must be planned with the needs of the local community in mind. There is no better basis for this than the direct involvement of the library staff in the everyday (and night) life of the community concerned.

There are certain obvious benefits which would be likely to accrue from any serious attempt at integrating the library service into the life of its immediate community. So far as the emerging

26

nations are concerned, such benefits, as Ken Gilmore points out in the final chapter of this book, are likely to be a long time in coming. However, if the kind of outreach experiment that is proving successful in many deprived areas in the west could be successfully exported to the third world, then the process of community development could be greatly assisted. Admittedly, there are all the problems of materials, staff, money and of course the problem of finding a suitable base from which to launch such projects however, one is talking here about the shoestring approach to outreach mentioned in the chapter on West Belfast. This level of approach is the very opposite of the ultra-gradiose projects still popular in many developing areas of the world, nevertheless they could form a possible future component in any attempt at development.

In the developed west, moreover, this kind of outreach project could well be of potentially greater importance, for on the outcome of such experiments could rest the future development of its public library service. Outreach librarianship is in essence an intensive form of reader-orientated library service, directed more often than not at the most reluctant of readers. If it should succeed then the entire question of the use and non-use of libraries, their relations with the public, indeed their very functions, will be thrown into the melting pot. Finally, a misallocation of resources lies at the root of many of the problems of our present day library service. if by the outreach approach the library resources of society can be spread more evenly over the whole of society then the fundamental social purpose of the public library service will have been realised.

REFERENCES

1 William L Ramirez 'Social concerns and the library' *California librarian* July 1969, 173-176.

2 L M Harrod *The librarian's glossary of terms used in the library and book trade and reference book* London, Deutsch, 1971.

3 Claire K Lipsman *The disadvantaged and library effectiveness* Chicago, American Library Association, 1972, 3.

4 Lawrence A Allen and Barbara Conroy 'Outreach librarianship, is it for you?' *Wisconsin library bulletin* Nov-Dec 1972, 389-390.

5   See John Colson's Chapter 4 below.

6   Organisation for Economic Cooperation and Development. Centre for Educational Research and Innovation *Strategies of compensation* ... by Alan Little and George Smith, New York, OECD, 1969, 37.

7   Michael Harrington *The other America* Baltimore, Penguin, 1963.

8   *Websters new collegiate dictionary* Springfield, Mass, Merrian, 1973. For a fuller version of this definition see Ken Gilmore's article below, Chapter 11.

9   Great Britain. Department of Education and Science. *Education circular 11/67* Aug 1967, 2.

10   *The Plowden report: Children and their primary schools* London HMSO 1967, argued that in certain inner city areas in Britain, educational provision was so poor in terms of staff, buildings and the needs of the children that they be designated Educational Priority Areas, and be given extra financial help to raise the standard of education to that prevailing in the country as a whole. See Joan Clegg *Dictionary of the social services* London, Bedford Square Press, 1971. Likewise, since 1969, under the Urban Programme, the special financial assistance has been available from central government for certain local authorities which contain areas of acute social need. See Clegg, op cit, 78.

11   Eric Butterworth and David Weir eds *Social problem of modern Britain* London, Fontana/Collins, 1972, 123.

12   United Nations. Department of Economic and Social Affairs *1970 report on the world social situation* New York, United Nations, 1971, 108-109.

13   Butterworth and Weir, op cit, 123.

14   United Nations. Department of Economic and Social Affairs, op cit.

15   Dudley Jackson *Poverty* London, MacMillan, 1972, 13.

16   Jack L Roach and Janet Roach *Poverty* Harmondsworth, Penguin, 1972, 23.

17   In 1959, the threshold of poverty established by the Social Security Administration was $3335 for a family of four. See United Nations. Department of Economic and Social Affairs, op cit. 127.

18   United Nations Department of Economic and Social Affairs, op cit, 109.

19 Clegg, op cit, 78.

20 Roach and Roach, op cit, 26-27.

21 Roach and Roach, op cit, 25.

22 Ibid. Note also that figures for the United States indicate that Federal expenditure on programmes designed to assist the poor increased from some 9800 thousand million dollars in 1961 to around 22 thousand million in 1968. Estimates indicate that the cost of maintaining one poor person between the ages of 17 and 57 can run to as much as 14 thousand dollars.

23 United Nations. Department of Economic & Social Affairs. op cit. This source discloses that in Britain in 1965, some 450,000 families or almost 3 million persons, that is nearly 4% of the total population was found to be living below the poverty line. 109-110. Another source lists the number of Americans living in poverty as ranging from 32 million to 50 million, or roughly from 19% to 25% of the population at the beginning of the 1970's. See Irving L Horowitz. *Three worlds of development,* New York, Oxford University Press, 1972, 222.

24 Western Europe has nearly 11 million immigrants who make up about 5% of the total population. See, S Castles and G Kosack *Immigrant workers and class structure in western Europe* London, Oxford University Press, 1973, 2.

25 For a concise picture of the complex of migratory movements see J Gould and W L Kalb, eds, *A dictionary of the social sciences* London, Tavistock Publications, 1964.

26 United Nations. Department of Economic and Social Affairs, op cit, 150.

27 United Nations Department of Economic and Social Affairs, op cit, 151.

28 The UN Department of Social Affairs does not recognise refugees as migrants, and it specifically excludes them from its definition. See, *Problems of migration statistics UN,* New

29 Castles and Kosack, op cit, 2.

30 United Nations Department of Economic and Social Affairs, op cit, 1.

31 Castles and Kosack, op cit, 1.

32 International Labor Office, Studies and Reports. Series N. (Statistics). No 18. *Statistics of migration* Geneva, ILO, 1932.

33 Castles and Kosack, op cit, 12.

34 Castles and Kosack, op cit, makes essential reading on this

point.

35   Clegg, op cit, 1.

36   Nicolas Deakin *Colour, citizenship and British society.* London, Panther, 1970. 22.

37   Deakin, op cit, 23.

38   Ibid.

39   British Association of Settlements. *A right to read; action for a literate Britain.* London, BAS, 1974, 4.

40   *United States literacy programs* Laubach Literacy Inc, Syracuse, New York, 19, 1.

41   United Nations. Department of Economic and Social Affairs, op cit. 198-199.

42   Golden, Hilda 'Illiteracy' *International encyclopaedia of the social sciences* vol 9, New York, MacMillan, Free Press, 1968, 412.

43   Ibid.

44   British Association of Settlements, op cit, 5. (Quoting the US National Reading Centre).

45   Golden, op cit, 414.

46   United Nations. Department of Economic and Social Affairs, op cit, 198.

47   Ibid.

48   Golden, op cit, 414. One is bound to point out, however, that the exact nature of this correlation is by no means agreed by economic historians, who argue over whether literacy is a cause or an effect of industralisation.

49   United Nations. Department of Economic and Social Affairs, op cit, 198. This source gives figures for 1970 illiterates in the world with a projected 800 millions by 1980.

50   Ibid.

51   Laubach Literacy Inc, op cit, 2.

52   Ibid.

52   Butterworth and Weir, op cit, 265

54   Butterworth and Weir, op cit, 266.

55   Butterworth and Weir, op cit, 267.

56   Butterworth and Weir, op cit, 262, point out that not only do many crimes remain 'unknown' to the authorities, but also that, in Britain, perhaps as little as one in six of all crimes known to the police are 'cleared' in a uniquely indentifiable way.

57   United Nations. Department of Economic and Social

Affairs, op cit, 223.

58   Ibid.

59   Ibid.

60   United Nations. Department of Economic and Social
Affairs, op cit, 224.

61   Ibid.

62   United Nations. Bureau of Social Affairs. International
survey of programmes of social development. New York, United
Nations, 1955. This shows that in the fiscal year 1951-52, the then
state of Pakistan spent about 6.5% of its total budget on its
police, courts and prisons.

63   United Nations. Department of Economic and Social
Affairs, op cit, 225.

64   United Nations. Bureau of Social Affairs, op cit, 144.

65   United Nations. Bureau of Social Affairs, op cit, 146.

66   See, European Committee on Crime Problems. Aspects of
the prison community Strasbourg, 1972. 1.

67   European Committee on Crime Problems, op cit, 3.

68   For a full discussion of this question see the European
Committee study.

69   United Nations. Department of Economic and Social
Affairs, op cit, 225.

70   Ibid.

71   In Britain, the BIT Information Service stands out as a
glowing exception to the lack of activity in this kind of area. See,
Library Association record 74, 6 June 1972, 99-100.

72   Kathleen Molz 'Past and present efforts at coordination of
library services at the community level' *Total community library
service,* report of a conference sponsored by the joint committee of
the American Library Association and the National Educational
Association. Edited by Guy Garrison. Chicago, American Library
Association, 1973, 65.

73   Ibid.

74   Molz, op cit, 66.

75   Allen and Conroy, op cit, 389.

76   Eric Butterworth and David Weir eds *The sociology of
modern Britain* London, Fontans/Collins, 1972, 58.

PUBLIC LIBRARY AND COMMUNITY DEVELOPMENT

GERRY FINNEGAN

Belfast community worker. Formerly a member of the
West Belfast Community Development Team

As mentioned in the previous chapter, the very word 'dis-advantaged' tends to be loaded with the accepted values of our present day society. For our purposes, 'disadvantaged' will be simply a term which covers those people or communities who are not catered for by the standard public services and for whom the need for public services is greatest. The term can apply equally in middle class or inner-city library catchment areas, because problems of alienation, loneliness and a general lack of community feeling, are as common as those created by boredom and increased leisure hours. However, for the purpose of this chapter we will direct our attentions to the problems of providing an effective and meaningful library service to those neighbour-hoods which may be described as deprived.

Community development has been applied in different social situations although most of the strategies have been used primarily in Asia, South America and Africa, in countries of the third world. Many of the points which follow develop from my own training and experiences in inner city situations, and have been adapted from lessons learnt in the third world. Although there has been little investigation of the social problems of large rural areas, or small to medium-sized provincial towns, many of the following points could be similarly applied to such areas.

The majority of urban connurbations in western society mush-roomed in the last century, with the great concentration of industry in the towns and the subsequent population movement, following the job opportunities from rural to urban areas. Our legacy as we move into the last quarter of the twentieth century, is a great number of densely populated cities; large areas of bad housing; areas of redevelopment; new estates and tower blocks; and highly automated industrial situations where job satisfaction tends to be a low-ranking priority. In addition, we now have increased leisure hours which allow people time to get involved in new interests and hobbies. With the present economic crisis we may find ourselves once again with a large section of our population unemployed, and consequently alienated, aimless, disillusioned and in need of purpose. I shall consider these urban areas of social need and social malaise, the fourth world, as it is now being termed, and the efforts made through community development to diagnose and treat many of the resulting ills.

How best can the public libraries be adapted to service these areas? Areas with substantial sections of the population to whom the library is an alien region, and the traditional services offered are seen as being unnecessary and snobbish. First let us look at those efforts being made by government departments and others to tackle the various social problems which now face western society. In recent years throughout the British Isles, many deprived areas have been singled out for preferential treatment by a government policy of positive discrimination. It is intended that areas of the greatest need receive the most attention. Throughout Britain, the Home Office has designated specific areas of social need as Community Development Project Areas, and a small team usually of professional community workers has been appointed to these deprived areas.

In the field of education, certain specific areas have been designated as Educational Priority Areas, thus receiving a greater allocation of resources. More courageous and experimental policies and approaches to the community's problems have been adopted by the local education authorities. In further education, investment in red brick universities is giving way to an expansion of the polytechnic idea which is something like two parts university, one part college and one part real life. However, these developments are only the tip of the iceberg, and are not typical of the level of provision in areas such as Northern Ireland. From a housing point of view there have been many recent efforts to deal compassionately with the proliferation of housing problems. The establishment of General Improvement Areas is seen as forming a slightly more humane alternative to the cold steel of the axe-wielding slum clearance and redevelopment man. So too in economic policy, it has been a customery approach of government to offer increased incentives to investors in areas of little or declining industrial activity.

Too often these problems are seen in isolation. Efforts have now been made to identify areas of social malaise. A recent survey of the greater Belfast area used seven indicators of social malaise: Unemployment, juvenile offenders, children in care, illegitmacy, infant mortality, general mortality and crowding.(1) The result after summing the 'scores' for each of the various criteria is a ranked table of social malaise in Belfast, ward by ward. Much of the information used in Boal's Report is taken from government statistics such as the census and unemployment figures, and, therefore, similar lists could be compiled for almost any area. Although these surveys have definite limitations, the perusal of such findings should indicate to any of the government's service agencies, including the library service, the kind of problems to be found in particular areas. Moreover, such data could be invaluable in the selection of sites, the design and layout of the building, and in efforts to gear the service to prevailing conditions in the community being served. In areas of overcrowding, a high number of people per household, the library would know to make provision for reading and study facilities where children and students could find peace to read and to do homework. Similarly, in areas of high umemployment, perhaps the library would do well to offering attractive and stimulating ranges of books, series of talks and films on useful ways of spending free time. Also the library could introduce various career and training opportunities, or provide information on alternative economic developments such as cooperative projects.

It may be said that Belfast is fortunate in so far as Boal's survey is available to all. Indeed since 'the troubles' in 1969, there has been no lack of research into many social aspects of life in Northern Ireland. However, without any such holocaust, the cities of Liverpool, Leeds and Glasgow have been the subject of similar research into social malaise. There is surely no shortage of social studies departments in universities, eager to apply themselves to the design and conduct of further surveys. It is important, however, that any such reports or surveys, including regular government statistics, should be utilised and not permitted to gather dust.

In the case of Boal's Report, the desired information was sought by the then Northern Ireland Community Relations

Commission (2) in an effort to identify defined areas of social malaise, so that a relevant community development programme could be carried out on the limited resources available to it. Community development it appears, was never really understood, or indeed perhaps its potentially far-reaching and almost revolutionary effects were understood only too well. At any rate, the Community Relations Commission and its independent community development programme, were abandoned despite inpassioned outcries from community groups.

Let us now consider what we mean when we use such terms as 'community work' and 'community development'. Three common factors in most definitions of community are:- a geographic area from which a community develops; a common sense of identity, hence community spirit; and an element of social interaction which binds the community together in some way. In practice the 'community' can cover such diverse groups as the European Economic Community, the Irish community in Britain, the business community of a nation, or the community spirit created by people living together in the same street, the same area or the same housing estate. Community work is concerned with trying to improve the lot of these individuals or small communities in disadvantaged areas, in an effort to create a better overall society.

Community work has itself developed into a generic term covering a large area of study and activity. To attempt in a nutshell, a definition of community work and what it is about, is a difficult and indeed contentious task. Generally speaking, practical community work can be said to be 'task' and 'process' orientated; involving tasks or material goals such as the building of a community centre; and processes, where in close cooperation with local people, the idea for say a community centre is developed and followed through to fruition. Community development, a specific branch of this field, tends to concentrate more on the educative aspects of the process approach. There are two main ways in which goals can be achieved when working with community groups; basically by a directive or non-directive approach. The directive approach is where a task is achieved for people, on their behalf; where for example, a community hall is provided for local people. Non-directive community development occurs where the local people themselves are involved in both the providing and the running of the community centre. The Christian

Aid slogan 'Give a man a fish and you feed him for a day, teach him to fish and you feed him for life', sums up very aptly the idea of community development.

As community development officers with the Northern Ireland Community Relations Commission, my colleagues and I loosely defined community development as 'a process which enables individuals and communities to use their own talents and growth potential to create a society in which they have access to resources adequate to meet the needs as identified at local level. In short the process attempts to bring the control of resources closer to the problems as identified by communities themselves, and, equally important, enables statutory and government agencies to be more effective and meaningful in the service which they provide to the community'.(3) Therefore, although the requirements of a community may appear self evident, community development should adopt a particularly sensitive approach to helping the community to achieve its goals. Again there is the problem of differentiating between the task and the process, and treating each separately. There have been many instances of community facilities, such as recreation halls, being presented to local groups only for the groups to find themselves totally unprepared for the responsibilities, chores and everyday practical problems of keeping such a community hall in operation. All this may be of great importance for someone involved in community work, but how can it be relevant to the work of a librarian? A look at the brief of a community development worker may show areas where his functions and those of the professional librarian overlap and where cooperation could develop to the advantage of both services. Both are involved in a general programme of community education. In Belfast a recently founded local community development project (4) has admirably summed up in its aims just what is hoped to be achieved through a CD policy. The project aims:-

1   To assist communities to effect fundamental change for the good of society.

2   To actively encourage participation in and shared responsibility for those resources and institutions within our society.

3   To relate these institutions and agencies to the needs of the communities and to foster cooperation between the communities and the agencies which serve them.

4   To provide a base for the training of community workers

and for the dissemination of information.

5   To promote research and evaluation into the methods and philosophy of community development and any other relevant areas.

6   To demonstrate to the statutory agencies the need for neighbourhood/community work and to show that it is as necessary as any form of community care, and to encourage government support for this work.

7   To provide formal and informal education as an integral part of the CD programme.

Were the goals of a library to be spelt out in this way, espcially of any form of outreach librarianship, they would not be too far removed from those of 'community development'. Obvious common ground exists where libraries can give practical support to CD programmes by providing an information service. Moreover, librarians should be broadening their concept of library service and building up relationships within communities. A great deal of work remains to be done in promoting the broad principles of CD within statutory agencies and services such as the library service. The task of the public libraries is to provide a relevant and meaningful library service to the public. In the case of disadvantaged areas, this will require the adoption of policies of positive discrimination with regard to the distribution of their resources. This could mean ignoring such guidelines as recommended library standards formulated as they are on a mainly quantitative basis. The 'process' in which librarians find themselves involved is concerned with how exactly public libraries provide and present their wares, and to what extent local people are encouraged to participate in both, the actual provision of the service and in saying what the service itself should be. If the library service has failed to reach large sections of its public then it should be prepared to accept constructive criticism, and by so doing, demonstrate its readiness to atone for past mistakes.

The library service must strive to build up relations with existing groups in the area which it serves, especially at a local or branch library level. It is in this area of outreach librarianship that some special category of community worker, community librarian or field librarian would be invaluable to a library. The problem would be straightforward if all that was required was for the library doors to be opened to all those who have felt out of things. This is not so, however, and consequently, a positive approach must be adopted, and people shown that it can be in their interests to come to a library. As a corrollory, the library must be willing to go to its public and publicise its facilities and resources through posters, local advertisements, the various media of communications, and by such methods as competitions for both children and adults. The government social services agencies now accept the fact that it is not sufficient to create benefits for disadvantaged people. The mere existence of these benefits is no guarantee that they will be taken up by the people in most need of them; people often have to be told of their rights. It is customary nowadays for change in social service benefits to be preceeded by a nationwide advertising campaign, both in the press and through the distribution of leaflets and posters by the statutory services agencies. Not only are the libraries in a position to cooperate with various government departments in the dissemination of relevant information, but also, they should be enquiring just to what extent the public's entitlement to a library service is being taken up by the disadvantaged groups in our society.

Librarians should be looking outward to community groups and the like, and asking themselves how best the rich resources of the public libraries could be of service to these groups. There are various ways in which the library can extend it's services by cooperating with locally based groups: by providing a library service to the senior citizens' lunch club; making rooms and resources available for adult education classes and seminars; by giving a new dimension to a 'night out' at bingo through having a selection of books available for borrowing, or perhaps by taking small collections to be placed in the local pub, working men's clubs or social hall. As well as extending the reach of the library service, such cooperation will help to increase the facilities which the many community groups can offer to their members, and to broaden the scope of activities. It should also encourage local people to make general use of common amenities and stimulate participation in the actual groups themselves. This can all lead to the creation of more active and representative community associations and to better rapport and cooperation between statutory agencies and the public. Furthermore, it could encourage, and even establish, the right of participation of local groups in some

38

organisational aspects of the library service.

Tenants and community associations are often set up as single interest/activity groups, individually giving priority to problems such as housing facilities, recreational amenities, redevelopment, unemployment or working with children and young people. These groups are faced with the many problems involved in trying to communicate with the bureaucratic jungles that seem to be so much a part of government departments. As their sights are seldom set very high, new horizons need to be introduced and avenues of communication opened up with the many statutory bodies. Particular emphasis should be placed on the passing on of relevant information to local groups, and indeed, a whole programme of informal community education must be undertaken. Frequently, to the disadvantaged, it seems that their problem is 'their's and no-one elses'. There is a role for libraries here both in the provision of such relevant materials as would encourage local groups to study and document their own situations, and by acting as centres for the exchange of such ideas and reports, whether drawn up by community groups themselves, or for the benefit and guidance of the groups. Through the library, and its range of community magazines, newspapers or newsheets, people could read of others in similar social situations. They could also be exposed to the inspirational activities of such champions of the disadvantaged as Cesar Chavez, Saul Alinsky, the Berrigan Brothers, Ivan Illich and Paulo Friere. Perhaps some of these works could be translated into a local vernacular and, therefore, become more significant in everyday living situations.

With so much still to be achieved in the field of community development in the 'fourth world' there is a need for the establishment of launching pads from which new ideas for solving social problems may be developed. Public libraries are an obvious point from which support can be offered to any all embracing social programme. Indeed, as centres for the dissemination of information and the exchange of ideas, libraries offer an ideal base to such a programme. The library could act as a focal point for a team approach to the problems to the disadvantaged, either as a base, or by offering its facilities and cooperating closely with community workers, social workers, teachers, youth workers, doctors, child guidance workers, community lawyers, trade unions, advice centres and the local people themselves. These public spirited people should be encouraged to use the libraries as a means of introducing their profession, explaining what it hopes to achieve and stating in what way they hope to contribute to overall community education and development. Not only could the library offer its own facilities but also it could share in the use of facilities elsewhere in order to provide a more total and comprehensive service to the community. Through the bureaucratisation of our society, people have become removed and isolated from central government, and such services as the legal system, originally set up to protect both individuals and society, seems more and more to be interested solely in perpetuating itself and alienating people by shrouding its workings in mystery and complexity. These abberations must be corrected, people and the agencies which serve them must be drawn closer together and comprehension must replace enforced ignorance.

Such well worn and popular techniques as exhibitions and displays, could be used by libraries seeking to focus upon certain aspects of community life. In conjunction with schools and playgrounds, or community workers and tenants groups, various displays and exhibitions could be presented with a view to increasing awareness in one's community and in society generally, for example, cooperating with schools for special courses of study, and with adventure playgrounds in introducing children to wide ranges of activities and interests. Community groups could be offered the opportunity of introducing their work and activities to a wider audience; to groups such as the boy scouts and girl guides, the pre-school play-groups and adventure playgrounds, single activity groups like football teams, and broader based groups like a tenant's association, mothers' club or senior citizens' club. Displays could be centred on the history and ongoing activities of one such group, and could include photo-stories, photographs, diagrams, slides and possible video-film, in addition to written reports and histories. The spotlight could then be turned on some of the general issues now facing society, for instance, housing problems, ecology or the alientation of the individual from the sources of power and control. Many alternative methods of solving social problems could be explored and presented in a simple and succinct manner by giving a platform to bodies such as trade unions, credit unions, claimants unions, womens liberation groups and such economic self-help projects as workers control and cooperative groups, housing associations and so on. Each of the groups invited would be encouraged to mount displays and to make future use of library facilities. This field could be even further developed with the dispatch of mobile displays to community centres, pubs and clubs, schools and elsewhere in the community. By getting to know these groups, by liaising on some of the points already outlined, the libraries would be in a position to be more sensitive to local needs and to adapt their services, down to the very books it supplies, to meet those needs as expressed at local level.

At this local level it is not enough to restrict these approaches only to democratically elected representatives, either of community associations or of other institutions in our society. The fact is that few community groups are as representative of their area as they would claim to be, and a certain anomaly arises as those people who are active in tenants groups are themselves generally more capable of articulating their thoughts than the average person in the community. To an extent this very ability separates these people from the communities of which they are a part. Therefore, the presence of community groups can in itself often be a buffer to actual communication between agencies and individuals if the agencies consult with them and them only.

So too a community of interest may or may not be formalised into an actual group. Efforts to attract the interest of a local footballing population could be made either by making contact with the local football teams; or by mounting advertising displays aimed at a broader audience, or both, whereby one may have an opportunity of contacting lads left out of the local 'super league' bracket, but otherwise interested in the game of football either as participants or observers. This practice can have a dual purpose - to the committed it can re-affirm already established interests and, to the unitiated, to a new and wider audience, diverse hobbies and interests can be introduced. There are many libraries where efforts such as these are being made, and from these small beginnings possibly a more relevant library service will emerge. In many areas and libraries, however, little or nothing has been achieved or attempted. From a community development standpoint recommendations can be made to the library service as a whole; recommendations based on the role of libraries as a support for community involvement, and as an integral part of community development.

Outreach librarianship must be seen as a sincere attempt to provide an adequate relevant service to all sections of society, and not simply as a gimmick to lure back lost readers into an unchanged environment. Librarians should support one another in their attempts to communicate their ideas within their own establishments and to the public as a whole. Administration often misinterprets or simply fails to understand exactly what is happening and what the needs are at grass roots level. Within the profession, it is important for librarians to both exchange ideas and experiences, and to actively seek criticism and objective views about their service from the community and others involved in the provision of social services. One recent example can perhaps be cited as an illustration of the importance of close links between the public libraries and the communities which they serve. The Belfast Education and Library Board was considering opening a temporary branch library until such time as the planned permanent library, could be completed as a part of an overall 'Whiterock District Plan'. Representatives from the library board met some local people and discussed the siting of the temporary premises and, in general, the boards' plans. Indeed the library authorities were very aware of the need for local support for and acceptance of their branch library. The area chosen, present troubles apart, is perhaps an ideal situation for the setting up of an experimental and responsive library service. Already there existed in the area three independently run community house libraries. So the potential was there to develop and strengthen the existing libraries and, possibly, to interest other families or centres to join a small network of home libraries, each with a stock of a few hundred columns, and with the focal point being the new branch library. In this case much of the onus of book lending could have been taken off the library itself and more time, effort and resources could have been left aside for other activities and more experimental methods of outreach librarianship.

However, the local library board, must have felt that their initial contact with local people, followed by press releases to the local papers, was sufficient. Rather than the local people nursing the library into its rightful position as part of the community, the temporary building suddenly appeared some six months later amid local whispers of 'Just what is it?'. Worse, during the weekend prior to its opening the building, books and other equipment were badly vandalised. No finger of blame can be pointed, accept at the vandals, yet there must be a lesson to be drawn from this example. The Education and Library Board was both courageous and positive as far as their decision to go ahead at a time of great upheaval was concerned, and pragmatic in as much as they saw the obvious expressed need for a library service and decided on an interim temporary building until such times as the planned new branch library would be serviceable. However, links with the community should have been already well established in the six months prior to the opening of the temporary library. This highlights the need for a team of field librarians and community workers, attached to the library service and liaising with the local communities, especially in such instances as the planning of new branch sites.

As can be seen, the practical problems which arise in the everyday running of the library service are many and complex. Many suggestions can be made with regard to providing the most amenable service. Although the question of censorship is a very sensitive one, no matter how subtle it is in practice, there should be some method of discriminating against certain reading materials, especially in relation to children in disadvantaged areas. This may mean a 'blacking' of unsocial or non-social reading material such as books which accentuate racism and sexism; those which indoctrinate children with absolute materialism from an early age, or with a belief that everyone holidays with their rich relations in an old castle; and books given up to the glorification of violence. These books should be put to the back of display cabinets and on the more out-of-reach shelves. One criticism often levelled at existing library services is that they are solely geared to serving the middle classes and to supporting the existing order. This image must be changed, the appeal of libraries made more universal, and the demand made upon them more far-reaching. Libraries could become centres not for revolution, as may be thought likely, but for changes which could eventually bring us to a more equitable and integrated society.

Moreover to an outside observer it would seem that much greater care should be taken with the contents of library book shelves, particularly in the case of branch libraries located in deprived districts. Too many libraries it would seem take pride in their standard collections, representative of all that is best in western history and thought. And yet how, space for space on each shelf, is a copy of Russell's *History of western philosophy* to be evaluated against say *George Best's book of football* or the *Film annual* containing pictures of the 'stars'? Again must the supply of classical records always predominate in music libraries, even when to a majority of the population such music is inevitably irrelevant? The importance of such materials, print and non-print is unquestionable but surely works of this genre ought to be located at central points, in reference libraries where they may be available to all who need them. They have scant claims to predominance in the average branch library, let alone the library serving the disadvantaged neighbourhood.

In the library situation, most casualties are generally the casualties of use and, therefore, money spent on books which are used can only be regarded as money well spent. The approach to the job, and the manner in which 'over-the-counter' transactions take place are often the only contacts which the user public has with professional librarians. Such an intangible item as approach can however, be so important in inter-personal contact. Librarians should be concerned, open and friendly, and not the stuffy and reprimanding people who have haunted many a childhood. The service itself must show a genuine effort in getting the library to the deprived, rather than expecting them to come to the library. In disadvantaged areas in particular, librarians should be positive, innovating and adventurous in aiming their service at as wide a public as possible. They must be wary of adopting patronising attitudes; and ought to be capable of accepting such rebuffs, as a few books stolen or damaged, and the odd broken window, without feeling betrayed. All aspects of the library service should be closely examined. Often psychological barriers can arise between the public and a statutory agency from the manner in which the service is provided. Again, whereas rules, regulations, fines, and the photographic filing machines which apparently obsess some librarians may be efficient, they often can be cold and clinical, and may in cases discourage potential users.

Having looked at ways in which the library can be of greater benefit to disadvantaged communities, it now remains to examine ways in which community representatives can participate in the provision of the library service. Methods and levels of involvement could include a users advisory committee, which could guide the library staff and introduce them to useful points of contact in the community. Another possibility is for a joint management committee comprised of community and library representatives. This alternative could pose problems owing to a tendency of such committees to formalise community potential by imposing a 'rigid model of participation' upon an unsuspecting community. The implementation of any such proposals would have to be preceeded by an acclimatisation period to enable both parties to 'learn the ropes'. The idea of a federation of community or house libraries serviced from a focal point, the local branch library, has already been mentioned. There may be many advantages in such a system. The service itself would be decentralised; it would come within the comprehension of a wider public; it would encourage and depend on community involvement and support; present staffing problems could be overcome by employing part-time community librarians, the job of lending books could be delegated to the house librarians and so much of the space and resources now tied up in unrepresentative and ineffective branch libraries could be released and adopted by other potential services.

The common ground shared by community development workers and librarians is expansive, yet the implications of this fact have not been realised or investigated to any degree. Like community development, librarianship can be seen as a profession having its own special purpose, in this case the provision of a service to the community. Moreover, as with other professions, the development of librarianship has resulted in a considerable apparatus of theory and practice which must inevitably complicate the relationship between libraries and the public. High powered cataloguing systems are every bit as academically relevant as is a detailed knowledge of say, group work in community development. However, the contribution made by these theories at library or community level can be questionable. It is important that both professions come within the comprehension of the people that they serve. So far as libraries are concerned, if they are to be relevant then they must undergo a radical change in role, a change in the general direction of community development.

REFERENCES

1   F W Boal, P Doherty and D G Pringle *The spatial distribution of some social problems in the Belfast urban area* Belfast,

Northern Ireland Community Relations Commission, 1974.

2 This independent agency founded by government in 1970 was phased out of existence in late 1974.

3 Community development and community relations in Northern Ireland: some proposals (Now incorporated into a folder of unpublished readings on community development in Northern Ireland).

4 PROJECT: Centre for Neighbourhood Development founded (1974) in Belfast.

TWO OUTREACH EXPERIMENTS IN WEST BELFAST

W J MARTIN

Lecturer, Department of Library and Information Studies.
Queen's University of Belfast

Until the last five or six years, Northern Ireland was a comparative backwater set on the fringe of western Europe, unfamiliar territory even to much of the United Kingdom of which it is a part. Recent events have changed all this, however, and the province and its problems have now become front page news all over the world. Unfortunately, it is violence and disruption that make news and so, depressingly little attention has been paid to those underlying social and economic conditions prevalent in the province for years and, arguably, a major factor in the current strife.

Nowhere is this more true than for West Belfast, for so long now a theatre for intercommunal violence, and yet, an area where for large sections of both communities, catholic and protestant, the winds of circumstance have blown almost equally cold. In West Belfast are to be found the Upper Springfield estates of the Northern Ireland Housing Executive, and two of the estates, Highfield and Ballymurphy, provide the background to the work described in this chapter. Lying on either side of a major road in the outer suburbs of West Belfast, both these estates are rigidly segregated, with Highfield being entirely protestant and Ballmurphy overwhelmingly catholic. Nevertheless, however necessary this neighbourhood segregation from the standpoint of individual security, its presence serves, somewhat ironically, to emphasise the tremendous similarities between the residents of these two socially-isolated estates, their life styles and their problems.

Ballymurphy is an estate of 650 houses built shortly after the second world war. It has a population of about 4,500. When it was built in 1948, there were considerable shortages of both skilled labour and building materials, and as a result the houses

47

possess neither pleasing appearances nor functional efficiency. That Ballymurphy was no great triumph for the planners may also be seen from the general lack of amenities obtaining on the estate. The shopping centre, comprising some six shops erected about four years after completion of the main body of houses, could never have been adequate, even before the savage vandalism which has reduced it to its present sorry state. From the outset Ballymurphy seems to have been an ill-starred estate. Originally planned to house people of both the main religions here, it rapidly acquired its present single creed status. It also acquired more than its share of 'difficult' tenants, often black sheep from other housing estates, and before long it was being described as a 'difficult' estate.

Not that this was entirely the fault of the residents, who were after all merely tenants, and moreover, tenants on an estate which had become something of a dumping ground for problem families. Moreover, the actions of the housing authority were not always seen to be taken in the light of objective social criteria and, rightly or wrongly, the tenants began to feel that if they did not themselves organise for the improvement of their estate then very little in the way of such improvement could be expected.(1) The outcome of all this was the initiation of a whole series of self-help projects, starting with the building of a community centre and leading on to the creation of employment opportunities through the medium of various local cooperatives. The list of these activities is impressive, indeed, all the more so in an area with few social amenities and a very high level of unemployment. It includes such concerns as Ballymurphy Enterprises, which is a knitwear cooperative, and Whiterock Industrial Enterprises, a builders' cooperative, with its associated venture the Peoples' Garage. There is also Whiterock Pictures, which produces block-mounted prints, a Craft Centre for the production of traditional craft goods, and Whiterock Industrial Estates, which is a collection of medium-sized factory units aiming to give employment to about 1000 people in all.

Highfield, built about the same time as Ballymurphy, is a larger estate of about 800 dwellings, mainly houses but with some flats and old peoples' dwellings. At present the estate is somewhat underpopulated for although 3500 people live in it, there are still many empty houses abandoned by their tenants during the 'troubles' in 1969. Serious efforts have been made to refurbish this damaged property, and a steady trickle of tenants to these homes has now begun. Many of these people are young couples from the immediate area, and there is now a strong tendency towards the reinforcement of already existing ties of community and kinship.

The amenity level on the estate is uniformly low, and were it not for the different slogans on the walls, the battered shopping centre could easily be the one at Ballymurphy. As at Ballymurphy, moreover, the residents have frequently found it necessary to fend for themselves, and the wooden community centre erected by the tenants' association is one result of their efforts. This community centre and the community house nearby, are the twin foci for a wide range of community based activities which include a youth club, a senior citizens' club, a tenants' association, and a library and advice centre. Each of these is itself the base for a host of related activities. Moreover, within the boundaries of the estate, local men are to be found, as at Ballymurphy, engaged on works of benefit to the community, such as the repair of damaged homes or the construction of all-weather soccer pitches. Some of these men are employed by the Northern Ireland Housing Executive, while others are involved in the Enterprise Ulster scheme, a statutory direct labour corporation aiming to provide employment on schemes of an amenity nature, and to recruit largely from the dole queues. It came into operation in September, 1973.

There can be no disputing the need for such efforts in two estates that could only be described as deprived. Indeed, while by almost any standards this description would apply, recent research into the distribution of social malaise in Belfast serves to emphasise not only this fact but also the essential similarities between the two estates.(2) Thus, on the basis of seven key indicators, Highfield was ranked seventh out of ninety seven Social Malaise Project Zones in the Belfast Urban area. Ballymurphy came sixteenth.(3) When every allowance has been made for the somewhat arbitrary choice of indicators involved, their limited range, and the uneven distribution of the various malaise factors between different zones, both Highfield and Ballymurphy remain as 'Multiple Problem Areas'.(4)

This was certainly the impression gained by the author on visiting both estates for the first time in late summer 1973. The

49

general untidiness and the evident vandalism made an instant and chastening impression, although on further acquaintance other and equally vivid impressions are gained, notably the friendliness of the people, and their courage and tenacity in the face of quite formidable difficulties, including the all-pervasive problems of violence and internment. Perhaps because these latter problems have tended to be more evident in catholic areas, and because the people in such areas came to believe that for them the self-help way was the only way, one had the impression that the community development process was more advanced at Ballymurphy than in the protestant estate across the way. At any rate the extent of local organisation, the quality of local leadership, and the solidity of purpose evident in the public support for community projects, inclined one to think in this direction.

In addition to the self-help measures already mentioned, Ballymurphy even had several voluntary 'libraries' in operation by the summer of 1973. The original Belfast Public Library service to the estate, which had consisted of a twice weekly visit by a 'mobile', had been withdrawn from Ballymurphy with the out-break of trouble in the area in 1969. Thereafter, the estate had no library service of any kind until several local people attempted to provide a voluntary service. Three notable examples of this kind of operation were, the library at the local curate's house, and two others run from private homes at different ends of the estate. Of these voluntary libraries, that operated by the local youth and community worker, Ciaran de Baroid, and his wife seemed particularly ripe for outside assistance for, not only did it have a sizeable membership but also, it was organised along quite impressive lines, with its own issue system and information facilities. The book stock was appalling, however, and one could not have failed to be moved by the sight of little groups of children patiently sifting their way through a collection of wornout and ill chosen volumes in the hope of finding something to read. One would emphasise, however, that this seemed an encouraging situation at the time, and one which could augur well for the eventual return of the public library service to the estate.

One would also point out that, although physically absent from Ballymurphy, the public library was by no means lacking in concern for the estate, and the library authorities readily agreed to the immediate deposit of several hundred new books at the home of the youth and community worker. The public library was also on hand with supplies of readers' tickets and shelving to another of the voluntary libraries on the estate, that run from their home by Sean and Jenny Quigley. Nor was this the only evidence of library intentions because plans were already well-advanced for the erection of a new £30,000 branch library nearby to meet the eventual library needs of the estate. Moreover, as an interim measure, a high-quality temporary library building of 2,700 square feet, housing a bookstock, adult and childrens, of some 17,000 volumes was scheduled for early completion.

Highfield once had a library of its own, a pleasant branch library of just under 1,000 square feet in area, with a bookstock of 6,000. Unfortunately, owing to the unwelcome attentions of vandals, this library, opened in 1958, was forced to close down in 1962. This left Highfield without a library service, apart from the mobile which called twice-weekly at an adjoining road, and which Highfield people largely ignored. A recent unpublished survey of library use in the estate conducted by the Highfield Community Centre, disclosed that some 4% of residents were regular users of this mobile, and a further 7% occasional users. The remaining 89% never had cause to visit the library. Despite such ill omens, one's immediate reaction upon arrival at the estate was a desire to get some form of library service going again. Even at that stage it was apparent that the kind of arrangements that would normally be covered by the term 'library service' would be of little practical value in the Highfield situation. It was clear also that direct personal intervention would be essential given the absence locally of either expressed library needs or voluntary provision. Hence, it was decided to 'nurse' Highfield in the hope that through a stimulation of demand, the conditions for the eventual return of the public library service to the estate might be created.

There were of course other and more pressing problems facing the residents of Highfield, problems so numerous as to endanger the very social fabric itself. The lack of amenities, the vandalism, the contempt for outside authority, and the sheer grimness of the environment all combined inexorably to place the library service at its proper point on the local scale of priorities. Modest as this placing would be in itself it was, however, linked to one really major priority towards which the tenants' association had been striving for some time, a return to some form of normality. Success in this aim would be marked by the reappearance of the normal, everyday appurtenances of life, and what could be more normal, any more ordinary, than the sight of a public library. Therefore, while never a major priority in itself, the provision of a library service was regarded as a positive step by certain of the residents of Highfield. Furthermore, such a situation seemed to afford a golden opportunity to assess the library's potential as a contributor to the community development process. Here was a chance for the library to become actively involved, and to cooperate with other public services and the local tenants' association in an effort to restore something resembling a normal social life to the area.

The community effort had already borne fruit in the shape of the community centre and the community house. This latter place, as its name suggests, is an ordinary terrace house, abandoned by its tenants during the 'troubles', and restored to serve as an advice centre and a point of contact for people in need of help. Space has always been at a premium in the community house, which in addition to its role as a 'storm centre' doubles as an office for Sandy Woods, the Highfield youth and community worker, and as the venue for innumerable meetings. Nevertheless it was decided to locate the library in the house because being such a popular meeting place for both children and teenagers, it appeared to offer the prospect of at least a readymade, if not exactly a captive audience. Moreover, as an American volunteer community worker was living in the house at the time, her presence it was thought, might deter would-be vandals.

The significance of locating the Highfield library inside the community house goes far beyond mere questions of security, however, and indeed, it would be hard to imagine a more logical or effective setting. The community house is one of the nerve centres of Highfield, a nodal point where community workers, residents, and visitors to the estate are in frequent contact. Therefore, not only does the library exhibit a high degree of 'visibility', but also it enjoys a measure of community acceptance hitherto unknown for any library in this area. This acceptance is a direct result of the library's association with the community house, and of its identification with the house's objectives. Furthermore, this is no mere 'marriage of convenience' but it is an organic relationship in which the community library has grown out of the self-help programme of local community development. The library could possibly survive on its own without the community house, but it would then have become simply another library instead of being the community library. The Highfield library is best viewed as an extension of the ideals of the community house, and as an attempt to unite community interest and potential with outside expertise for the common good. This in large measure means a recasting of the basic library idea in the mould of community needs, and it will be possible only to the extent that members of the community can be persuaded to participate. As this participation develops there should be a gradual transition from what is at present a broad, multi-activity self-help project towards a single-activity venture, a genuine community library. This library will exist to provide ordinary people with the kinds of information that they need, and it will be organised for this purpose. Consumer information, news of job openings, changes in the public transport system or in the public services as a whole, and data on matters of social welfare, the law and basic civil rights will be made available, as will the kind of recreational materials on demand within the community.

The Highfield library opened its doors in October 1973, and by its nature, rendered extremely unlikely any comparisons between it and the average public library. In the first place, with a volunteer staff of two, and a stock of around 300 second-hand books it was by all accepted standards completely inadequate. Moreover, in any normal library situation, the premises themselves would have been dismissed out of hand, comprising as they did one rather ordinary council house with a basic 'library' floor area of about 200 square feet. As for the furniture it was strictly functional and, consisting of a faded three-seater settee, an ancient dining table, and four rickety chairs, could just as strictly have been defined as minimal. Nor were there any shelves for the books, which we attempted to distribute invitingly at strategic points around the room, as much in an attempt to make them appear more numerous as anything else.

Into these surroundings poured our first batch of readers and in this unprepossessing setting they quickly made themselves at home Those early scenes at Highfield strongly resembled those at Ballymurphy with groups of eager youngsters vying with each other for the privilege of borrowing some tattered volume. One point, however, was inescapable. No matter how inadequate the library may have been from the standpoint of accepted levels of provision, in the context of a deprived community it was demonstrably effective. Indeed, those aspects which elsewhere would have assured its imminent demise were at Highfield a source of great strength. It was rundown, ill-equipped, draughty, and vaguely impermanent in character. It was, in other words, like almost everything else in the local environment.

Originally, the library opened for only one afternoon a week, but even at this the demand for books was so great that fear of inundation forced us to look for outside aid. This was readily forthcoming from the Belfast Public Library, which, after an initial and unsatisfactory attempt to supply us from the nearest 'mobile'. agreed to the placing of deposit collections at the community library. With the advent of these new books most of our original stock was consigned to the rubbish bin, although some of the paperbacks and more lurid novels were retained for the use of teenagers, and of the few adult visitors to the library. The overwhelming majority of our members, however, are children and young people, and the bookstock reflects this fact. Picture books, easy readers, annuals, stories for boys and girls, and a suitable range of non-fiction comprises the bulk of our stock. On arrival these books were arranged on shelving specially made for us by the boys of the local secondary school.

This improvement in the book supply situation led almost immediately to other improvements, notably in the range of services offered by the library. The staff of two, myself and the American volunteer Kate Cullinan, was joined by my colleague Rosemary Jackson who, in addition to helping with the everyday routines began to take story hours in an upstairs room. A request service was introduced and this proved to be so popular that it was soon found necessary to integrate it with the public library request system. A good supply of request cards is kept on hand and, where possible, readers are asked to fill them in personally, as this helps both to take some weight off the staff and to bring people with writing difficulties to our notice. The request proceedure is the nearest we come to having a normal library routine, at least so far as the readers are concerned. The issue system comprises nothing more than a series of book pockets filed in reader order, one pocket containing cards for all the books currently on loan to each reader. There are no fixed loan periods and no fines are charged. There are no other rules as such, and rowdiness, unruly behaviour, even a certain amount of horseplay, are accepted without comment in an environment where, after all, such things are commonplace.

The membership continues to grow, as does the bookstock. We now have approximately 1000 volumes in stock, and a readership of around 400. Most of our members are in the age group 7 to 14 years, with the sexes being fairly evenly represented. There is more than one way of 'using' a library, however, and some of our members do so without even borrowing a book. Highfield is not a good reading area, and a fair number of our customers would have to be described as 'slow readers'. For these children we try to provide both materials, in the form of easy readers, and reading practice, by having them read to the staff and to other library members. A recent development has been the appearance at the house of a senior remedial teacher from the local education authority.

It cannot be overemphasized that the Highfield Community Library exists neither to inculcate the reading habit nor to nurture future members for the public library service, although both are benefits which could accrue from the experiment. It is primarily a community development project in which the library and its outreach approach are seen as potential stimuli to local attempts at self-improvement. To this end a great deal of emphasis is put upon direct personal contact with the readers, and this is maintained through conversation with individuals, group discussions, participation in handicraft and cookery sessions, and by taking photographs of the readers and recording their voices on tape. These latter activities are especially popular with the 7 to 14 year-olds, who greatly enjoy performing before the camera and the microphone. It was indeed their enthusiasm for such pursuits that prompted our most ambitious effort to date, the making of a videotape.

For many of our members, the main attraction of the library lies in its lively and friendly atmosphere. This applies particularly to the teenagers who come to the library in the evenings to meet their friends and drink coffee. Very occasionally, one of them may borrow a book, but it is much more likely for them to ask for something from our tiny record collection. Books are an unattractive prospect to these unliterate young people, (unliterate in the sense that although having a certain command of literacy, they do not choose to use it any more than is absolutely necessary), and the major thrust of the library so far as they are concerned will have to be in the direction of non-print materials. As yet, however, one is talking about the future. For the present, teenage readers and the small but growing band of adult callers at the library, can choose from a selection of about 100 paperbacks and perhaps 200 hardbacks in the 'light fiction' bracket. To develop this aspect of the service, a more extensive provision of paperbacks, complete with modern display stands, is planned.

Now almost eighteen months old, the Highfield Community Library is today a flourishing enterprise. The library proper is open on three afternoons a week, but being part of the community house, its facilities are available at virtually any time. The positive nature of local response to the library could scarcely have been anticipated, and, indeed, all the signs had been that at Highfield the establishment of even a community-based library would require a prodigious effort from all concerned. At Ballymurphy on the other hand, the signs had been more encouraging and, in consequence, one's expectations somewhat higher. With the benefit of hindsight it is clear that these expectations were unrealistic. As for the decision to concentrate one's efforts upon Highfield and leave Ballymurphy to its own capable devices, this, while basically sensible, was to place a heavy burden on the shoulders of the Ballymurphy volunteers. Certainly, Highfield was in need of priority treatment at the time, but then so was Ballymurphy, its local initiative notwithstanding.

At any rate, with the Belfast Education and Library Board's plans for the area already well-advanced, to say nothing of the problems involved in finding a suitable building on the Highfield model, it was decided that support for the existing voluntary libraries be continued pending the erection of the proposed temporary branch.

In the meantime the activities of the Ballymurphy volunteers intensified, particularly at the library run by the youth and community worker, which before long was opening for two afternoons a week and attracting an ever-growing membership. For a time in fact, this growth in membership reached such proportions that the membership had to be closed to enable the volunteers to cope with the numbers calling at the house. Like its counterpart at Highfield, the Ballymurphy library is situated in an ordinary terrace house. There too the aim is to keep routine procedures to a minimum, and to make the library the kind of place that people really want to visit. The membership is of a similar composition to that at Highfield, being comprised mainly of boys and girls in the 7 to 14 age group. They read very much the same type of material, and respond to the same kinds of encouragement. The Ballymurphy library is, however, situated in a family home which means that readers do not have quite the freedom to rampage around that they do at Highfield, which is no more than a 'pad' for the resident volunteer. At Ballymurphy, on the other hand, the staffing situation has always been a litle bit easier, with as well as the De Baroids, a reasonable supply of student teachers willing to help out in the library. Undoubtedly, the Ballymurphy library has been a success. Whether measured in terms of reader response, local community reaction, or the stimulus given to the statutory authorities by the force of voluntary example, it cannot lightly be dismissed. Paradoxically, however, those same factors which go towards making the library so effective, its informality and its voluntary character, are also the source of one of its major weaknesses, the absence of any direct professional involvement. Therefore, although the volunteers do a sterling job in providing a basic lending service, this service is limited to a considerable extent by their lack of professional expertise. Hence, such refinements as request and interloan facilities are missing, as are the story hours which are such a regular feature at Highfield. Moreover, the revision, updating and general exploitation of the bookstock is much more evident at Highfield than at the Ballymurphy library.

Not that any criticism is intended of either the Ballymurphy library or its hardworking volunteers. If failure there has been it was failure on one's own part to fully appreciate the facts of the situation. Both these libraries were founded on cooperation between voluntary workers, community organisations and the public library. Without this cooperation, and the community support that flowed from it, neither experiment would have been successful. However, for this cooperative formula to work to best effect, all the elements in it need to be present, and at Ballymurphy the factor of professional expertise was missing. Hence, one would argue, that library has not attained quite the same degree of development as has its counterpart at Highfield, where all these factors have been present. Moreover, communication between the several elements involved in the Ballymurphy library has on occasion been hindered by conflicting interpretations of the situation on the ground. Thus at times the seemingly luke-warm response in official circles has caused severe frustration among the volunteers. Quite clearly, having been without a library service for a considerable time there were occasions when they tended to see the situation in terms of 'people versus officialdom'. To the outsider, however, once official recognition had been given to these voluntary efforts, the Ballymurphy library was viewed as a 'holding operation' pending the return of the public library to the area. Clearly such ambiguities can spell danger for any community action project and, given the history of community relations in Northern Ireland, much more attention should have been paid to this aspect.

It would be wrong to exaggerate either the difficulties encountered in the operation of these two projects or the differences between them. They are, after all, both practical examples of the outreach approach, and both show that outreach ventures can be undertaken at a very modest cost. Indeed, this has been outreach on a 'shoestring'. In the last analysis, however, the importance of all such experiments will, so far as many librarians are concerned, be judged by the extent to which they influence the mainstream of public library practice. At Ballymurphy, the prospects now appear to be quite good, with Belfast Public Library just about to resume its activities in the area. An earlier opening was arranged but unfortunately, just before this could happen, the temporary library building that was to be the first phase in a renewal of service to the area, was vandalised. This caused disquiet not only in library circles but also within the local community, where it was felt that with better use of community contacts this need not have happened. Once the official service gets fully underway, the position of the voluntary libraries will have to be re-examined. They will most probably revert to their original role as contact centres and meeting places, while perhaps continuing to serve as a form of 'half-way house' between the reluctant reader and the public library. It is to be hoped, nevertheless, that the lessons of the voluntary experience will not have been lost on the public library. At the very least, one would look for a continuation of the process of community involvement, embracing everything from the employment of local staff at various levels, to the operation of some form of local users sub-committee. At Highfield, there is as yet little indication of any planned return by the public library service to the estate. There, it is proposed to continue with the operation of the voluntary service, and indeed, in some quarters the return of the municipal service would be regarded as something of a mixed blessing, given the appeal of the community house library. In fact, suggestions have already been made for the opening of a second community library within the estate, on the grounds that no official service, however indulgent, is capable of providing anything of comparable relevance to the needs of the residents. This remains to be seen, and no matter how understandable such sentiments may be, one is mindful of the considerable assistance given to the Highfield project by the Belfast Public Library.

As regards any insights which may have emerged from the West Belfast experience, one would certainly stress the factor of impact. One of the most obvious criticisms of both these libraries would be as concerns their minimal impact on adults and teenagers. The explanation for this probably lies in the fact that, although both libraries are very much service-orientated places, they still to a large extent exist to serve readers. How much more is this true for the average public library? If libraries are to be places only for the reading public then only the reading public, or part of it, will use libraries. Admittedly, librarians today are much more aware of the value of non-print materials although, arguably, the provision of these media is often based on a desire to improve services to existing users. However, if the library service is to be genuinely orientated towards serving the entire community, then the needs of non-readers will have to be taken much more seriously.

In the last resort it all comes down to the essential purpose of public libraries. If libraries exist to meet the expressed needs of a minority of the public then they can continue to operate along traditional lines. However, if they are really intended to serve all of the public then an extra dimension to the library service is going to be required. This extra dimension could possibly be provided by allying the outreach approach to the professional expertise of librarians, and by bringing both of these to bear upon the social problems of the day. Disadvantaged people have shown their willingness to accept the public library in those cases where the library has demonstrated that it does have something to offer. Unfortunately, however, it is often libarians themselves who are most in need of assurance on this point.

The lessons of West Belfast are clear. If the public library service is to have any hope of becoming relevant in deprived areas, then it must be prepared to become involved with these areas, with the people who live there, and with their problems. Community cooperation and support are vital to the success of any library project with the disadvantaged, but knowing who the people are, finding out what it is that they want, and pitching the service at a relevant level are every bit as important.

REFERENCES

1 A E C W Spencer *Ballymurphy: a tale of two surveys* Belfast, The Queen's University, Department of Social Studies, 1973, 4.

2 F W Boal, P Doherty and D G Pringle *The spatial distribution of some problems in the Belfast urban area* Belfast, Northern Ireland Community Relations Commission, 1974.

3 Boal et al, op cit, Appendix 4, 126. The seven key indicators were:- male unemployment; infant mortality; bronchitis deaths, children in care; illegitimacy; male juvenile offenders; crowding.

4 Ibid. This shows that with a male unemployment rate of 33.3%, Ballymurphy was ranked first in all 97 zones for this factor. Highfield came 22nd on this one.

THE UNITED STATES: AN HISTORICAL CRITIQUE

JOHN C COLSON

Formerly Assistant Professor in the University of Maryland, School of Library and Information Services. Currently teaching at the University of Chicago.

1. 'Outreach' and 'library service to the disadvantaged' have been principal slogans of public librarians in the United States during the 1960s and 1970s, used to reassure each other of their 'relevance,' even their necessity, to the good order and health of the republic.(1) New words, however, often obscure old concepts, and the current popularity of 'outreach' does that. The public librarian in the United States has long held a strong sense of his mission to serve the unserved. Indeed, Melvil Dewey or Frank Hutchins or Lutie Stearns would have said that any American without easy assess to a public library is disadvantaged.(2) The attitudes they expressed have been so strongly shared by American librarians that from the founding of ALA in 1876 to the enactment of the Library Services Act in 1956, the principal goal of public librarians was to make their institutions available to every citizen.

Nevertheless, from that beginning in 1876 there have been public librarians advocating use of the public library for improving availability. In one way or another they have emphasized the need for librarians to reach out and become engaged in the lives and aspirations of Americans less fortunate than the typical public library user. Many late nineteenth and early twentieth century public librarians advocated use of the public library for improving the fortunes of a wide variety of the disadvantaged — in ways not too much different from arguments by librarians of the 1960s and 70s. The examples cited here are not intended to be exhaustive nor definitive — merely representative.

In 1899 E E Allen was arguing a greater effort by public libraries to meet the needs of the blind.(3) A L Bailey, in 1907, advocated the public library's responsibility to the 'working man' — the 'deserving poor' of the early twentieth century.(4) By 1911 the condition of millions of immigrants in America was a matter of increasing concern to librarians such as F C H Wendell.(5) At the same time Arthur E Bostwick and others saw the public library as a significant source of support for the settlement houses and other agencies working for the uplift of the urban poor.(6) Institutionalized children also became a source of concern to public librarians.(7) Here and there, especially in the cities of the 'new south,' public librarians even were beginning to turn their attention to black people in America.(8) In northern metropolitan areas the new problems of industrial, urban life were beginning to attract attention from librarians, and the 'urban information specialist's' advent was forecast by the work of J Ritchie, Jr.(9) The criminal element, too, was seen as susceptible to the good works of librarians.(10) And N E Dodd professed to see the library as an effective deterrent to organized prostitution.(11)

The benevolence and sincerity of these spokesmen cannot be doubted, but their efforts were to be engulfed by the corrosive fires of world war one. American librarians turned from their benevolence, and adapted readily to the tasks of defeating the Hunnish monster. The lamp beside the golden door was turned off, and the disadvantaged became objects of suspicion. 'War work' became the watchword of the ALA, and thousands of American librarians filled the ranks, soldiers in the Army of the Righteous: 'Ours is a humble yet glorious service in showing our people that while our country is made *safe* for democracy, each individual must be *made fit* for democracy.'(12)

World war one was a turning point in American public librarianship; the social concern evidenced in the materials cited above declined significantly. There appears to have been in the postwar decade a general retreat into the safer problem of extending library service into areas without public libraries. The establishment of new institutions — a process of vigorous development begun in the 1890's — continued; in 1930 the *ALA directory* accounted for 5,364 public libraries. On the other hand, the development of 'outreach' services appears to have abated. ALA's concern for 'Americanization' became a matter of 'work with the foreign-born,' with emphasis on providing immigrants works in their native languages. Even so, the reports of the ALA round table on work with the foreign-born reveal within the association a decreasing emphasis on service to the immigrant. By the mid-1930's ALA attention to the matter can only be described as perfunctory.(13) 'Outreach' services to the blind continued to be improved, but this was achieved largely through the organized efforts of the blind which resulted in increased appropriations from the congress to the Library of Congress Division for the Blind, established in 1931. Prison and other institutional libraries were also a matter of relatively static concern within ALA.

In the 1920s public librarians developed a renewed emphasis on service to the individual. The most sustained outreach program was the reader's advisor movement, which in effect was an attempt to install in the public library a tutorial system of adult education.(14) It was in many ways a magnificent attempt to bring the public library into an actual status as the 'people's university,' but its emphasis was squarely on the individual reader who already believed that the public library had significant value for him.(15)

The advocates for the readers' advisor service saw in the concept a means by which they might reach the 'men and women who cannot or will not join study groups or classes but who will follow systematic courses of reading.'(16) The readers' motives might be purely vocational or purely aesthetic, but librarians saw them as serious-minded individuals to whom were owed a special obligation, by helping them to develop 'that satisfaction and inspiration which comes with accomplishment or mastery.'(17) The American Library Association developed an elaborate set of rationalizations for the program, 'reading with a purpose.'(18) At the core of the service was the fundamental idea that the principal responsibility of the readers' advisor was to assist readers to a level of development which would enable them to continue their self-education independently of the advisors. The program was one which seemed to promise eventual fulfillment of George Ticknor's pledge that the public library would be the 'crowning glory' of the public schools. It was a movement which gained strength throughout the 1920s, despite the many complications and contradictions in American society and American librarianship which militated against success.(19)

Whatever might have been, we shall never know. Under the hammer of the great depression, 1929-39, the readers advisor service was beaten into new form, and advisors to readers became consultants to organizations outside the library.(20) And, with the advent of world war two the reworking of the service was completed. A remark in the *71st annual report* of the Chicago Public Library epitomized the transfiguration: 'Advising readers is now the least of the functions of the readers' advisor, whose time is chiefly devoted to labors with a large implication, but constituting as a whole a valuable contribution to the public and professional relations of the library.'

In the conventional view the years of depression and war were a traumatic period for American public librarians. Certainly, there were difficult times for many of them, especially in the depression era of slashed salaries and disappearing budgets for books and other materials. But the record is mixed, and development continued along some lines. The number of public libraries continued to increase, although at a rate sharply reduced from that of 1876-1920. Within the ranks of public librarians professionalization appears to have developed strongly, and educational programs for public librarians continued to progress along the lines laid down in the Williamson Report. The history of American public librarianship, 1923-1945, is largely unwritten, but it seems fair to state that at the end of world war two the public librarians of the United States were poised uncertainly for the future, eager to continue their record of development but with some apprehension about a re-descent into the worst times of the depression — a mood shared with the rest of America.

The apprehensions vanished slowly under the impact of post war prosperity, but by about the mid-1950s it was apparent to public librarians that their age of affluence had indeed arrived. Everywhere in America, it seemed, the public library was flourishing as never before. Everywhere, established insitutions were getting glittering new buildings; everywhere, new public libraries or branches were being founded; everywhere, city or county library systems were developing into a reality beyond the dreams of Melvil Dewey and his disciples.

Those dreams were no longer adequate, and the public librarians of the 1950s responded to their new prosperity with ambitious proposals for development. Demand for public library services was outstripping the ability of American cities to meet it, and the ALA was able to mobilize the demand for achievement of a long-held wish: direct federal support for the public libraries. In 1956 the congress passed the Library Services Act.

In 1956 the American public library movement reached a significant turning point. During eight decades of development the movement had come increasingly under the direction of professional librarians, especially those offering leadership through the American Library Association. The record of their leadership remains unanalyzed in many significant aspects. Even without the support of studies based on the record, however, it seems fair to assert that in 1956 many, if not most public library promoters and advocates regarded their mission as nearly complete. The Library Services Act seemed to promise fulfillment of the old dream of making effective public library service readily accessible to every American. The act was widely regarded as a triumph of democratic aspirations. Public librarians' eighty years of effort in the extension of their services could be said to have been their major 'outreach' program. Thus their mid-century achievement was a basic justification for their optimism.

This optimism, verging on complacency, pervaded the profession. The decade after world war two was one of considerable introspection in the profession, and in a series of major documents about librarianship, public librarians and their associates demonstrated a strong concern about professional problems, but little interest in the society for whose benefit they existed. The documentation of unconcern is a difficult task, but there are indicators from which one may infer that from 1945-1960 and beyond there was in American public librarianship disinterest in the dispossessed. For a public librarian to advocate the use of the library in amelioration of social problems was to invite censure. Joseph L Wheeler, doyen of American public librarians, wrote in 1946 of the 'confusion' among his colleagues, and identified the principal cause for it: 'the socially minded librarians, who are deeply concerned that their libraries give greater attention to social, economic and political problems.'(21) Ernestine Rose, a pioneer in outreach programs, wrote in 1954 of the divisions among public librarians with respect to the 'so-called social field.' (22) Beneath the controversy about the social issues lay the assumption that the public library was meeting the needs of society. In 1957, at the University of Chicago's Graduate Library School Conference, 'New directions in public library development, Philip M Hauser spoke of the demographic changes occurring in the American city, and adverted to their effect on the public library. Noting the shift of black people from the rural south to the urban north he foresaw only that 'the library undoubtedly is contributing' to their transition from a rural to an urban way of life and would continue to do so.(23)

The chairman of the conference drew upon Hawser's remarks to relate the American black's future use of the public library to that of the immigrants of 1880-1915.(24) Statements like those by Wheeler and Rose were only straws in the winds of progress. The absence of social concern in their major testaments is the real test of public librarians' complacency, even into the 1960s. The list of those negligent documents is a formidable one, but the attitude is epitomized in a major textbook on public library administration, published in 1962: 'This chapter title ("A program to serve the whole community") may be called unrealistic, for probably 30 per cent of the population in any community are too young, too old, mentally undeveloped, irresponsible or lacking in ambition and intellectual curiosity for any educational or cultural service whatever'.(25) Sixty million Americans were thus written off as unable to derive any benefit from the public library.

2. Among the American people there has always been one group whose presence has been a continuing reproach to the ways in which we have put into practice our manifest destiny to liberate the world from tyranny and enlighten it for the responsibilities of democracy. Coming here as chattels less valued than cattle, for more than three centuries they endured the status of invisibility and served, like the idea of sinners in the church, as apostrophes to our virtues. Even the darkness of their skin served our neglect, enabling us to hide them in the shadows of the American dream.

As it was with the American people, so it was with American public librarians. From Franklin to Jewett to Wheeler, public librarians ignored the existence of the black American. The occasional Frederick Douglass or Booker T Washington was celebrated as proof for our democracy, but into the twentieth century public librarians seemed unaware of this dispossessed segment in our society. Perhaps they assumed that if public libraries were everywhere available there would be no problem of service for this underclass.

In 1913 William F Yust did raise the question: 'What of the black and yellow races?'(26) There was a response from the profession, but during the next decade it was a feeble report of isolated successes in organizing some sort of library service for black Americans here and there. For example, during the period 1914-1920 only eight such articles are listed in the *Bibliography of library economy,* and four of those were published in non-library journals.

In 1922 the American Library Association gave a measure of official recognition to the library needs of black Americans. They allowed the establishment of the 'work with negroes round table'. It survived two years, and in 1923 issued a series of optimistic reports on 'progress,' north, south and west.(27) Then the round table disappeared. Considered from the perspective of effectiveness, the round table barely merits attention. Its members achieved nothing in the way of extending public library service to black Americans, nor does it appear that they attracted even the passing attention of the American Library Association. They did, however, leave a record which brilliantly illuminates the unconcern of American public librarians for putting their institutions where they said their hearts were.

In preparing for the 1922 meeting of the round table, Ernestine Rose sent a questionnaire to 122 public libraries:

1   What percentage of your population is negro?

2   Have they free access to the library?

3   Have you any specialized equipment for serving them, such as a) Separate colored branch? b) Colored assistants? c) Special book collection on the negro and negroid subjects?

4   If you have negro assistants, what methods have you for training them?

5   In what way is the negro represented on your governing board?'(28)

Replies were received from 98 libraries, and the responses, tabulated in the proceedings of the round table reveal starkly the feeble presence of black people in American public librarianship. There was, for example, only one professionally trained black librarian in those 98 libraries. Nor did blacks have more than token representation on public library boards: A characteristic answer to this question is 'We make no distinctions of race or color. There are no "special classes" represented on the board'.(29) In the south there was more concern about the problem than in the north, and from the Atlanta Public Library came a reply which illustrated the southern side of the problem: 'We tried having an advisory committee from the colored people but as they did not confine their activities to advice, we disposed of them'.(30) Ernestine Rose summed up the situation: 'library work for negroes is still largely a thing of the future.'(31) She also issued a little noticed prophecy to her colleagues. In a 'talk on segregation' she 'spoke of the north as coming rapidly to face a problem similar to that of the south .... Legally, colored and white are on the same ground, but in many cases there is not a real feeling of equality in the library.'(32)

In the next two decades the situation described in 1922 did not change significantly. For example, for the period 1921-1932, *Library literature* includes only twenty-seven entries under the subject heading *Negro and the library*. The New York Public Library's Harlem Branch was celebrated as an important center in the 'Harlem renaissance' of the 1920's, but the example it offered shone all the more brightly because of the darkness around it. In 1936 the American Library Association issued its report, *Libraries of the south; a report on developments, 1930-1935*. Chapter VIII: 'Library service to negroes,' consists of eight pages written in the hope that things might get better. In 1944 Gunnar Myrdal's *An American dilemma* set forth the reality of public library service for American blacks: 'In a few southern cities, such as Nashville and Richmond, upper class negroes are allowed to use the white library if they sit at a special table or in a special room. Inter-library loans from the white to the negro library also improve the situation in some cities. In the north there is no segregation or discrimination in the use of these facilities, except that created by residential segregation and the unfriendliness of a relatively few white officals and members of the public.'(33)

Myrdal's findings only describe the situation as it existed toward the end of world war two. Their meaning was best expressed by Eliza Gleason a year later. Her article, 'Facing the dilemma of public library service for negroes,' appeared in the October 1945 issue of *Library quarterly*. Briefly she recounted the progress which had been made since 1900 in extending public library service to black Americans. It was negligible. Unable to take comfort in her own report, Gleason advocated abandonment of the public library and urged black communities to seek public library service through contractual arrangements with the libraries of the black colleges in America, especially in the south. Considering the pathetic condition in which those institutions existed, there can be no greater measure of the despair black Americans felt about asking white public libarians to begin to make good on their promises.

Their despair was not unfounded. During the next decade and a half, the situation was not altered significantly although the journals of the library profession began to report more efforts at redress of black grievance about public libraries. Using the good offices of a variety of agencies, black communities did succeed in obtaining a few more libraries and some improvement of services. The inadequacy of all this, however, was still such that at the end of 1962, Virginia Lacy Jones (Dean of the Atlanta University Library School) could still cry out, 'How long? Oh, how long?'(34)

3. In the decade to come the further development of the public library occurred within a society which appeared to be rending itself. Multitudes of black Americans seemed to come suddenly to the decision to take direct action against the sources of the misery and degradation in which they found themselves. Their example excited the imagination and fed the courage of other aggrieved groups in the nation. Resistance came easily to those who would maintain the status quo; direct action led to reaction. What had been a legal struggle became a physical struggle as briefs were replaced by brickbats. Riot and tumult, mayhem and assassination became everyday events of the news. In the streets and the executive suites Americans confronted one another in angry contention about the imperfections in our democracy, what to do about them, and how to do it. Through all the controversy there came a developing public purpose to correct the social inequities in American life and a concurrent conviction that the federal government was the only agency with sufficient prestige and authority to superintend the task of building a better America — a great society, as President Johnson put it. He opened a war on poverty and urged (and drove) the congress to a series of notable declarations: the Civil Rights Act of 1964, the Voting Rights Act, the Economic Opportunity Act, the Higher Education Act, and others. As part of the war on poverty, the Library Services Act of 1956 and 1961 was revised into the Library Services and Construction act. It and the Economic Opportunity Act became

the principal supports for a resurgence in public library development.

It may not be possible yet to sort out and categorize all the responses to this new opportunity for public librarians to revive their sense of mission. The 'profession' did not react in unity and what may be viewed as an incoherent response may also be seen as a result of growing diversity among libraries. By 1950 it was no longer possible for Americans to define precisely a 'public library.' For example, we could not even count them: in 1950 the US Office of Education reported 6,028 public libraries in existence; in 1951 the American Library Association reported 6,416 plus 2,364 branches of 508 public library systems.(35) If the two organizations in the US most concerned with public libaries are unable to arrive at an accurate count of them, how can it be possible to define 'public library services?'

Be that as it may, the availability of federal revenues prompted a great variety of public library programs under two rubrics: 'outreach,' and 'library service to the disadvantaged.'(36) Whatever words were used, the programs had two purposes: to enable librarians to participate as librarians in the effort to ameliorate or eliminate the causes of poverty and ignorance in America, and to bring the poor and underprivileged to a state where they could make effective use of the public library's resources for self development. These activities were as diverse as the imaginations of those who conceived and executed them; they were also as diverse as the kinds and amounts of resources available to the program planners. Some were conceived with little imagination and established on the proverbial shoestring. Other were grandly conceived and operated in what amounted to an embarrassment of riches. An attempt to describe just the various kinds of programs would not be helpful. Those cited here are presented only to indicate their variety. The County Library of Multnomah County, Oregon, put into effect a children's services program for the migrant workers' camps in the county.(37) The Brooklyn, New York, Public Library (which has a long record of 'outreach' services) was an early entrant in the war on poverty with its district library program, an attempt to put libraries in closer touch with neighborhoods.(38) In a Rochester, New York branch library Richard Moses used motion pictures to attract non-readers into the library, and he stressed the film as a communications medium which did not need to be tied to books.(39) In New Haven, Connecticut, the Public Library and Community Progress, Inc, established the New Haven Public Library Neighborhood Center — a 'social or neighborhood center built around books and ideas,' but which also featured toys, games and manifold cultural activites.(40) In the San Francisco Public Library, Guy Bennette and others introduced the concept of the 'street librarian' — a librarian who dispensed books and information from a box of books on a car parked at curbside.(41) The New Mexico State Library established a statewide program of 'out-reach' service to American Indians.(43) In King County, Washington, school officials, librarians and juvenile court administrators collaborated in a program to provide library services to children in custody of the King County Juvenile Court. (43) For all of the diversity in the details of these activities, there was a common thread of purpose behind them. It is the same purpose which animated the work of Dewey and Hutchins and Stearns, but is best restated, perhaps, in the words of Meredith Bloss, Director of the New Haven Public Library: The NHPL Neighborhood Center came to be, partly, from, 'The conviction that when people know the facts, they're more apt to make a better life for themselves. A skillfully collected and usefully organized collection of books can become an active force for good in the community when aggressively and imaginatively exploited.' (44)

Neither Dewey nor Hutchins nor Stearns nor any other public librarian in American would disagree with that. Still, the state-ment comprehends the ambiguities and contradictions inherent in American public librarianship, and it is in those matters that we must search for solutions to the problems of the public library in America. The sense and the pride of mission have not been adequate to the need.

The inadequacy began to be apparent almost from the begin-ning of the 1960s rebirth of outreach. Wheeler and Goldhor, for example, were not content only to write off the 30 per cent of the population who could not benefit from the public library. They expressed concern about the '25 to 40 percent of the population, especially among adults, which does not yet use the public library, but could be enouraged to read, study and seek information on their multitudinous personal interests. To draw (them) into the circle of library use is priority item 1 in any library's program.'(45) In the same year Dan Lacy of the American Book Publishers' Council dramatically underscored the point with his suggestion that if one per cent of the people of the city of 20,000 went to the public library for information on a specific subject, the first dozen people would exhaust the library's ability to meet the demand.(46)

American public librarians' first skirmishes in the war on poverty were mainly attempts to meet the needs of the disadvantaged by aggressive exploitation of the libraries' collections of books. Books, however, were only the standard weapon of the librarians. They also used other materials — sound recordings, especially of popular music, motion pictures, paintings and sculpture, toys, games. Nor was the effort confined to materials; in many libraries there were determined attempts at turning library programs into events which would convince the disadvantaged of the values of library use — into significant 'happenings' to use the argot of the day. They were set into motion by convictions of the kind stated by Meredith Bloss: that use of the public library can be a significant factor in the disadvantaged individual's climb upward from his status. The belief is strongly held by most public librarians in America; for all of that, it is but a variant of the traditional American belief in the idea of the ruggedly individual self-made man who lifts himself to success by tugging at his own boot-straps. The librarians' version of the concept is a gentler one than that advocated by followers of Spencer and Sumner, but in the end it comes down to the same thing. It is also just as much an abstract principle, of chiefly mythical value.

Public librarians' participation in the war on poverty also was based in a concern for self protection. It was generally admitted in the profession that, for whatever reason, somewhat more than half of the adult population did not use the public library.(47) Thus the attempts to promote public library use by the disadvantaged were strongly influenced by a desire to promote the use of the library, per se. Programs intended to assist the disadvantaged were in fact designed to attract non-users into the library, without much regard for what might happen to him once he arrived. 'Just show the movies — never mind the books!' proclaimed one advocate for outreach. 'it's the latest — it's the greatest — it's the lib-er-ee,' shouted another.(48)

The blare and glare of the deodorant huckster were used to 'sell' the library as program directors made extensive use of advertising and public relations techniques. The advertising and publicity were aimed at convincing the disadvantaged non-user that he needed the public library in his efforts to remove from himself the burdens of despair, discrimination, oppression and poverty. Perhaps so, but the disadvantaged remained unconvinced.

It became apparent that the programs, promotion, and publicity had made only a marginal difference in the use of the public library by the disadvantaged. In a society whose 'priorities' increasingly were coming to be determined by the impact of numbers it was becoming apparent also that the 'numbers' were not accruing to the advantage of the public library. The non-users remained non-users, or, in the brief eloquence of Milton Byam, despite all the concern, despite all the promotion, 'Nothing happened.'(49)

As the decade began to wane, spokesmen for the disadvantaged began to deliver an unqualified message of disdain for the public library. At a National Library Week celebration at the Smithsonian Institution in 1968, Anthony Campbell, an assistant to Washington, DC Mayor Walter Washington, delivered a scathing attack on the public library.(50) There were other such messages. Perhaps the cruelest message came from John M Cloud, himself a black man and a librarian. In the riots in major American cities during 1965-68, according to Cloud, black people did not burn the public libraries within their reach, because the people were utterly indifferent to the libraries.(51) In that same spring a stronger shock was administered. On 10 February 1969 the Newark City Council voted to close the Newark Public Library, a nationally prestigious institution since the first decade of this century. After vigorous, almost frantic intervention by librarians, chiefly through the state government, the city council reversed its decision a month later. The most significant thing about the whole matter is that the Newark City Council had for more than a year been involved in bitter dispute between its black and white members, and the Council was almost paralyzed. Yet, on this matter the black and white elements were able to act together in relatively easy harmony.(52) Nor have the shocks abated since then. Early in his second term President Nixon announced that for fiscal year 1973-74 he would not request any funds under the

Library Services and Construction Act, to the dismay of few Americans other than librarians and their friends. The congress did not accept the idea, but LSCA funds were reduced substantially, and the issue is not yet entirely resolved.

4. Since about the advent of the twentieth century (and especially since the great depression of 1929-39) American society has appeared to be subject to great, sudden changes in mood and manners. Public librarians and their institutions, a microcosm of America, have given a similar appearance. Indeed, in the record of public library development since 1900 there is abundant evidence with which to document a charge of excessive mutability, not to say faddism. The charge would be inaccurate, even unfair. Despite the appearance, especially despite the labels, public librarians have applied to their activities — 'readers' advisor service,' 'Americanization,' 'adult education,' 'extension,' 'out-reach,' 'library service to the disadvantaged,' and others — they have been motivated by a deeply held sense of mission, to make the advantages of books and other materials available to all Americans. If we look behind the labels it is possible to see the continuity between Melvil Dewey's certainty of his 'high calling' and Meredith Bloss' 'conviction.' That it is also possible to see the public library, as a 'cold, elitist' institution is somewhat beside the point. The phrase is only another label.

Nevertheless, it must be said that public librarians have not succeeded in their mission. It may have been an unrealistic mission from the beginning; All Americans may neither need nor want the materials in public libraries.

The fact that many Americans do not desire direct access to public libraries and their contents has been abundantly demonstrated. Public librarians and their associates, however, have continued to assume the need; and have further assumed that Americans who do not use public libraries act against their need. Those are propositions which have never been proved. Further, they stem from a profound misunderstanding of society, one in which it is assumed that social needs are distributed uniformly among the individual members of society. In this belief it is also assumed that those needs can be met by the design and distribution of standardized agencies on some per capita basis. This set of ideas leads towards the establishment and maintenance

74

of agencies which are bound to be dysfunctional in modern American society.

America is not what it was two centuries ago, and the gross measures of increase in population, territory and wealth - which we use in our attempts to understand American 'growth' actually servce to obscure more significant qualitative changes in American society. The relatively simple, pastoral society of 1776 has been replaced by a tremendously complex urban, industrial society. Moreover, it is a society which uses technology to maintain communication among its scattered components. The use of these technologies of communication has led to the establishment of many new kinds of communities in American society, communities not known in the period when American society took what is still its basic form. There is good reason to believe that the form is no longer functional. The unitary society for which our political forms and institutions were designed no longer exists.(53)

American society is beset by a number of serious problems, and it has become a cliche to say that the problems result from a breakdown of community. That, however, is not true. What has happened is that we have been given many new ways in which to organize new kinds of communities, without regard to spatial limits. Neighborhood communities in many cases have been seriously damaged, perhaps beyond repair. William F Whyte's *The organization man,* with its attention to the 'problems' of Park Forest, Illinois, offers a classic illustration of the process — and an equally classic case of misunderstanding of it. The 'organization man' is caught in a profound dilemma. On the one hand, he is powerfully bound to a new kind of community; on the other, his family must exist in a 'village' where the sense of community is declining rapidly, despite frenetic efforts to maintain or restore it. At the other end of the scale is the Frontenelle family in New York City. They are seriously disadvantaged, according to the conventional measures of advantage; those disadvantages are compounded by the fact that the Frontenelles live without community — they must attempt to live without the support of communal concern and understanding, on such nominal 'assistance' as an indifferent welfare bureaucracy can muster.(54)

All along that continuum of society, Americans suffer from a similar problem: most of our political and legal concepts of community are still tied to the neighborhood frame. The manner in which we devise our representation in government, for example, is seriously dysfunctional because the representatives are chosen from territorial jurisdictions rather than from communities, be they aldermen or senators. In order to gain the attention of their nominal representatives many of our communities must resort to extrordinary measures: bribery in the case of affluent communities (the Associated Milk Producers, Inc, for example), or riot in the case of the disadvantaged (the black people of Watts, for example).

Community has but one base: communication. Where there is no communication there is no community, despite all of our attempts to insist otherwise. Communities organize themselves on the base of people in communication about common interests. If they have the opportunity to develop, communities will also establish and maintain institutions appropriate to their needs. In eighteenth century New England, for example, the residents of the towns had a high incidence of common interests, and in each such community there were only a few individuals whose particular interests transcended the borders of the towns. In our society there is great diversity of interests, and many individuals within a particular . jurisdiction — county or town, city or state — have interests and needs unrelated to those of their neighbors. Many people belong to several communities, each organized around some set of interests. Our technologies of communication and our methods of community organization make it easier, in some cases, for national communities to maintain themselves than for those organized as a result of propinquity. Many of our people, however, are compelled to exist outside the shelter of communities — such as those in prisons — or in accumulations of people who are cut off from effective contact with other communities — such as the 'invisible man' of Ralph Ellison. Too many black Americans must live in 'neighborhoods' in which the larger society works to prevent community development. So it is with too many Mexican-Americans, too many American Indians, too many Puerto Ricans, and with too many other hyphenated Americans, for that matter.

This is the true measure of their disadvantages. Their poverty, their illiteracy, their crime, and the rest of their social disorders are the result of their status as men without community. When these dispossessed begin to establish their own communities and to lead their development, the social disorders will be ameliorated, as those new communities begin to deal with their own problems.

and to take care of their own members, as communities have always done. To permit those without community to develop it, and to regulate the conflict of interests between communities are major tasks confronting American society.

5. Libraries are derivative agencies. They rise from particular needs within society, and their forms and functions tend to reflect the diversity within the society. Thus, in the United States there is an amazing variety of libraries, one which greatly transcends the usual typology of academic, public, school and special libraries. (55)

One type, at least — the public library — is frozen in the same mold in which it came into existence nearly two centuries ago. It has two principal attributes: it is supposed to serve the entire 'community' in which it exists; and it is established and maintained under the control of a board of 'representatives' from the same 'community'. (The usual number is seven or nine; it is seldom more than fifteen.) This form and purpose were developed in the rural communities of New England in the eighteenth century.(56) That the same form and purpose should be in effect two hundred years later is but the result of our continuing to define community in the same way we did then. (The same may be said of other institutions in American society, such as schools, hospitals, even universities.) The most serious result, of course, has been that as the number of Americans has increased and as their interests have diversified, the public library has become increasingly remote from the communities into which Americans organize themselves. In all but the smallest cities of America the public library trustee cannot possibly 'represent' the myriad communities in them. Nor can the library staffs bridge the gap — at least, not as libraries are presently organized. Librarians tend to respond to their professional colleagues rather than to their users. (Again, the same may be said of other professional groups, such as educators, physicians, even professors.) The public library is an anachronism. It was designed to meet some needs of the community in which it developed. It was one result of a long period of community development, but it appeared just at the time when American society was beginning to undergo profound and far-reaching changes. Rather than a foundation, the Boston Public Library was a culmination, soon to be made obsolete.

In its present mode the American public library is irrelevant to many communities in American society, precisely because public librarians have identified their mission as service to individuals rather than service to communities. Communities have their own information systems — networks of communication — and they establish mechanisms whereby information necessary to the communities can be acquired and distributed through these channels. The Massachusetts Historical Society is a classic example of such a community and mechanism. Established in 1791 to serve a limited community, it survives, a 'public library' which serves with distinction a limited, specialized community. (The London Library, to wander afield, is a similarly classic example of the same thing.) There are thousands of such specialized 'public' libraries in America. Of greater importance to public librarians, there are thousands of communities without public libraries because a society which sees jurisdiction as community is unable to accommodate to legitimate communal claims against the public library.(57)

The 'disadvantaged' also see the public library as irrelevant, not because they are indifferent to their needs for information, education and other benefits which can be obtained from libraries, but because they lack the communal connections by which they might begin to organize themselves to meet their needs. The elimination of this lack is a task beyond the abilities of public librarians — it involves the entire society. There are, however, legitimate supporting roles public librarians can take in this task. When nascent communities can be identified, public librarians can support their leaders in the effort to organize the communities and prepare them for the political struggle necessary to gain effective admission into this great society of communities. The work confronting public librarians is two-fold: 1) To re-organise their institutions in order to serve the communities without libraries, 2) to re-organise their activities in order to assist whose without community to organize their own. The work is not beyond the wits of public librarians; it should not be beyond their will.

REFERENCES

1   See, for example, Fern Long, 'Library service to adults: work in progress' in: Kate Coplan and Edwin Castagna, eds,

The library reaches out (Dobbs Ferry, N Y,: Oceana Publications, 1965), 163-86.

2   See, for example, Lutie E Stearn 'The great unreached and why' *Wisconsin Library bulletin* 24: 270-75 (1928).

3   'Departments for the blind in public libraries' *Public libraries* 4: 171-73 (1899).

4   'How shall the library help the working man?' *Library journal,* 32: 198-201 (1907).

5   'Stranger within our gates: what can the library do for him?' *Public libraries* 16: 89-92, 121 (1911).

6   'Social work of the St Louis Public Library' *Library journal* 36: 461-65 (1911).

7   Grace Chute 'What a library can mean to an institution child' *Minnesota Public Library Commission notes* 4: 1-3 (1913).

8   G T Settle 'Good reading for negroes. I: The Louisville Free Library' *Southern workman* October 1914: 536-40.

9   'Anent the Boston Co-operative Information Bureau' *Library journal* 40: 397-99 (1915).

10 'Making convicts into citizens' *Wisconsin Library bulletin* 11: 132-34 (1915).

11 'Library versus the white slave traffic' *Library journal* 37: 508-09 (1912). These early attempts at outreach have not yet been adequately studied. The best paper on the subject is Wayne E Jack 'Station number eleven of the Enoch Pratt Free Library' *Journal of library history* 7: 141-56 (April 1972).

12 Irma M Walker 'The library an Americanizing factor on the range,' *Wisconsin Library bulletin* 14: 209-13 (1918). Emphasis in the original. Walker was Librarian at the Biwabik, Minn Public Library.

13 See the reports of the round table in the 'Proceedings' number of the *ALA bulletin* 1920-37.

14 John C Colson 'The reader's advisory service: an experiment in adult education' Ms paper in the possession of the author.

15 See, for example, Carl H Milam 'The educational service of the library' *Wisconsin Library bulletin* 18: 79-80 (1922).

16 'Organized adult education service in libraries' *Adult education and the library* 1:3: 1-10 (25 December 1924), 2.

17 'Reading courses' *Adult education and the library* 1:4: 1-33 (May 1925), 4.

18 American Library Association. Commission on the Library

and Adult Education *Adult education and the library* 5 volumes, 1925-30.

19 Some measure of these problems can be taken from the *Annual reports* of the Chicago Public Library, 1924-33. The Chicago Public Library was the scene of one of the most ambitious readers' advisor programs in the United States.

20 Library Association of Portland *71st annual report* (Portland, Ore, 1935) p 21; Jennie M Flexner 'Books and advice, '*Journal of adult education* 6: 188-91 (April 1934).

21 Joseph L. Wheeler, *Progress and problems in education for librarianship,* (New York: Carnegie Corporation, 1946) 14-15.

22 Ernestine Rose *The public library in American life* (New York: Columbia University Press, 1954) 106.

23 Philip M Hauser 'Community developments and their effect on library planning' *Library quarterly* 27: 255-66 (1957), 260.

24 Lester Asheim 'Summary of the conference' *New directions in public library development* (Chicago: University of Chicago: University of Chicago Graduate Library School, c1957), 100-01.

25 Joseph L Wheeler and Hervert Goldhor *Practical administration of public libraries* (New York: Harper and Row, c1962.) 23.

26 *American Library Association bulletin* 7: 159-67.

27 *ALA bulletin* XVII: 275-77 (1923).

28 *ALA bulletin* 16: 362 (1922).

29 *Ibid,* 363.

30 *Ibid,* 363.

31 *Ibid,* 363.

32 *Ibid,* 366. Emphasis in the original.

33 2 vols, (N Y, Harper and Brothers, C1944) I: 634.

34 *Library journal* 87: 4504-05 (15 Dec 1962).

35 US Office of Education *Bulletin* 1950, no 9; ALA *Directory* 1951.

36 This phraseology itself is of uncertain meaning. In *Library literature* for example, the following entries were among those used, during 1960-1971, to identify public library programs of the nature discussed here: Negro and the library; Reading — special groups of readers; Public libraries — services to illiterates, — services to groups, — services to the foreign-born, — services to negroes; Public libraries — metropolitan areas; Libraries and social and economic problems.

37 Ruth McConnell and Frances Postell 'Books Roosevelt Grady' *Library Journal,* 89:3384-86 (15 September 1964).

38 Milton S Byam 'Brooklyn Public Library's district library scheme' *Wilson library bulletin* 35: 365-67 (January 1961).

39 Richard B Moses 'Just show the movies — never mind the books' *ALA bulletin* 59: 58-60 (January 1965).

40 Meredith Bloss 'Responding to manifest needs' *Library journal* 89: 3252-54 (15 September 1964).

41 Guy Bennette 'San Francisco: down these meaningful streets' *Wilson library bulletin* 43: 872-75 (May 1969).

42 William H Farrington 'Statewide outreach: desert booktrails to the Indians' *Ibid,* 864-71.

43 E F Klepeis 'King County Youth Service Center: a case study in library cooperation '*Library journal* 98: 1359-63 (15 April 1973).

44 Op cit, p 3252.

45 Joseph L Wheeler and Herbert Goldhor op cit, p 23.

46 *Library journal* 89: 3274 (15 September 1964).

47 Wheeler and Goldhor's two categories of non-users, for example, add up to a total of 75% of the total population. The circumstances in which their estimate was published incidate its general acceptance.

48 Richard B Moses, op cit; and Pauline Winnick 'It's the latest; it's the greatest; it's the lib-er-ee' *American education* 3: 5-7 (June 1967).

49 Mary Lee Bundy *Metropolitan public library users: a report of a survey of adult library use in the Maryland Baltimore-Washington Metropolitan area.* (College Park, Md, University of Maryland, School of Library and Information Services, 1968); Milton S Byam 'Public library services in the inner city' in Miles M Jackson, Jr, ed, *Comparative and international librarianship* (Westport, Conn, Greenwood Publishing Corp, c1970), 47-62; Kathleen Molz, 'The public library: the people's university?' *American scholar* 34: 95-102 (Winter, 1964-65); Eric E Moon 'What is happening to public library circulation?' *Library journal* 91: 3851-63 (1 September 1966).

50 Reported by Priscilla Dunhill 'Dust gathers on the public library' *Reporter* June 1968, pp 34-36. The writer was present on the occasion; Ms Dunhill's report of Mr Campbell's remarks is an inadequate summary of them.

51 John M Cloud 'Overdue: why didn't they burn the libraries?' *Wilson library bulletin* 43: 787, 812 (April 1969).

52 The episode has not been adequately studied by librarians.

Wilson library bulletin 43:787, 812 (April 1969).

52 The episode has not been adequately studied by librarians. There is horrified reporting of it in the journals of librarianship, and better reporting in the *New York times*. It is given perfunctory — and entirely misleading — treatment in John E Bebout 'Partnership federalism' in: Ralph W.Conant and Kathleen Molz, eds, *The metropolitan library* (Cambridge, Mass, The MIT Press, c1972) 80-82.

53 On this point see also: Melvin M Webber 'Order in diversity: community without propinquity' in Resources for the Future, *Cities and space: the future use of urban land* ed by Lowdon Wingo, Jr (Baltimore: The Johns Hopkins Press, c1963) 23-54.

54 Gordon Parks 'Harlem family: the Frontenelles' *Life* 64: 48-63 (8 March 1969).

55 This variety is not adequately recognized, even in our library education curricula, a condition which contributes to perpetuation of this obsolete categorization.

56 See Jeremy Belknap's remarks on the 'social library' in his *History of New Hampshire* (2d ed, Boston, 1813) III: 247-48. The type of library of which he wrote was the direct antecedent of the 'modern' public library.

57 Linda Crowe et al, 'If they could solve the (library problems in Champaign-Urbana, they'd have the solutions to the world's problems' *Wilson library bulletin* 47: 283-89 (November 1972).

THE WHY AND HOW OF OUTREACH: REACH OUT OR BE FORCED OUT

JENNY ARMOUR

Formerly employed as Special Services Librarian
with the London Borough of Lambeth

In Great Britain it is often said that half to three-quarters of the population rarely or never uses a public library. Yet as ratepayers they are compelled to contribute to its maintenance and must be assumed to be unwilling to claim their rightful service, or else they are unaware that they have rights. One would suggest that many people are ignorant of services available because even those libraries which do advertise just do not reach everyone.

Therefore the librarian must reach out into the community in order to serve this section of his population. If he does not make time to do this, the library service will surely fade and die. At a time when national borrowing statistics are falling steadily(1) in spite of many libraries increasing the number of books each reader is permitted, the library cannot afford to be seen as totally irrelevant by more than half of the population. National pressure on local authorities to reduce public expenditure will mean that councillors looking for cuts will deal harshly with a service that is used by less than half their voters. Add to this the fact that the public library service is now a statutory service for all who need it(2) and it becomes apparent that it is the librarian's duty to take steps to present the service to all non-users.

The librarian who cannot face such blatant selling of the service is not really a public librarian. His feelings are more in line with the academic or research librarian whose users make clear demands for him to satisfy. The outreach librarian has to be an ambassador. He also to succeed, has to have maturity and understanding, and very deep concern. He needs to care, and to provide a caring service with will sometimes be intensely personal. He will be able to identify latent needs and to determine how best to serve them. He will also be an enthusiast and a keen salesman.

But let us consider what he is selling. Books or libraries? They are not the same. Chichester librarians recently sported 'Libraries are fun' T-shirts,(3) but libraries in themselves are not fun. Libraries are places where books (used throughout this essay to mean all materials used by libraries) are stored until they are required. Libraries are also buildings where other things may happen, according to local need and the layout of the building. It is books which may be described as fun. They may also be described as important, necessary or useful, according to the particular book and its impact on the reader. So the librarian should be selling the idea of books first, demonstrating their relevance to the people he is reaching out to, the people who will not go into a library. Only secondly is he selling the idea of a library as a possible place to go for a variety of activities, pop group to political meeting, practice room, darkroom, do-it-yourself workshop, which happens to make books available as well.

Where does the outreach librarian begin to look for his invisible clientele? Every district varies, but take the London Borough of Lambeth as an example. Lambeth is one of the twelve Inner London boroughs all of whom share some of the deprivations of inner city areas, in common with the central areas of other large British cities such as Birmingham, Manchester, Liverpool and Glasgow. Lambeth librarians attempt to offer a service to a resident population of 300,000 as well as to a large daytime commuting population drawn into the office and industrial developments in the borough.

In an inner city area it must be recognised that there is deprivation of every kind and merely to exist from day to day is an achievement in itself. Where housing is overcrowded, insanitary and often in a ruinous state; where education is of the poorest sort and pretty irrelevant too; where families are incomplete; where alcoholism and violence thrive; where incomes are lowest, unemployment highest and daily life is drab; is it surprising that books and libraries have a very low priority?

And yet, think how important they could be. Think of the picture books which would introduce a slum child to rich colour, and the thrill of escaping, however temporarily, into an absorbing story. But the mother of the child we are talking about is very likely to be undereducated and unaware of what her child lacks. She is likely to be struggling to make ends meet, struggling to keep clean a house which is long past repair, struggling to keep her children healthy in the face of powerful environmental odds. One third of all British children are disadvantaged(4); they will fail to develop their potential, fail to thrive physically, and fail in school. The whole quality of life will be different for these children and they in turn will become parents with poor employment prospects, little stamina, poor health, and lacking the ability to survive the competitiveness of modern society. Their children are more vulnerable before they are born. The mothers lack contraception, pregnancy information and advice, so many have too many children. They then lack the income and knowledge to buy a nutritional diet, and they seldom get guidance in child care.

The obvious answer is to change society. However, while we wait for this to happen, there is much that librarians should be doing in the way of interim measures. Take illiteracy as an example. When the educational system improves to the extent that it no longer releases some twenty percent of its sixteen year old school leavers as functional illiterates, and when everybody who is over sixteen and who wants to read has learned this skill, then there will be no need for libraries to provide simple reading materials for adults. But there can be no argument against such provision at the present time when possibly three million Britons are either totally or functionally illiterate. To cite a recent analogy (5) the swimming pool contains, as well as a deep end, a shallow end, water wings and life-savers. Should the librarian provide less?

In Lambeth, in addition to the thirteen branch libraries, a mobile library service pays short visits every week to some thirty sites in 'backwater' areas where although not necessarily far from a library, the residents are mainly non-users. This mobile service has proved to be more successful in attracting readers than was the service operated from the existing branch libraries. Although one can criticise the formality of the Lambeth blue paintwork, it is less imposing than the usual library building and, because of its size (2000 volumes) it tends to be more intimate and inviting. The stock is deliberately popular and contemporary in tone, and the staff, who are outreach minded, work from among the books and not from behind the desk. Moreover, the absence of fines on overdue books has proved to be particularly popular, especially with those people who had previously used another library.

What about those who use neither branch libraries nor the mobile service? Some because of physical handicap are unable to use the library and amongst this group, the greater proportion of whom are also elderly, will be found some avid readers. It should be possible for ambulances from social services or from task force to bring some disabled people to the library from time to time, as happens regularly in Camden,(6) and thus supplement the traditional books-on-wheels service. The mentally handicapped have often been dismissed when library provision has been considered, but it is a fact that the severely sub-normal can enjoy the experience of recognising objects in a picture-book, and that those less handicapped are able to enjoy more complicated illustrated books, and can make enthusiastic use of colouring books and pop records - both items which it should not be beyond the powers of public libraries to provide. With the development of training schemes, more and more of the mentally handicapped are learning to read, and will increasingly need the simpler reading books currently being provided for adult illiterates. One of the Lambeth libraries serves as the base for a reading club for educationally sub-normal teenagers. As this type of activity spreads, librarians will surely welcome the use of their buildings by a group that has more often than not been excluded, at least implicitly. Those in training centres can be brought to their library individually or in small groups at frequent intervals, and parents can also be encouraged to bring along their mentally handicapped son or daughter, whether child or adult.

In the context of library service there is often some confusion between the mentally handicapped and the mentally ill, although their needs are in fact quite different. Whilst the mentally handicapped form quite a small proportion of the total population, every second family is likely to have a member who is mentally ill at some time. The mentally ill are more likely now than ever before to be out patients, or to attend day centres and live in the community, either with their families or in hostels or grouped flatlets. People who are mentally ill may find great comfort in reading, and there are some psychotherapists who take bibliotherapy very seriously. Whilst one would not insist on any form of separatist library provision for the mentally ill, it can be valuable for librarians to contact hospitals, day-centres and hostels, as well as the local branch of MIND, (National Association for Mental Health), to learn what in these circles would be considered an optimum library service for their needs. Such service may include the provision of deposit collections, the holding of book promotion or discussion sessions, or perhaps the hosting of an art exhibition.

Amongst others who may feel shut out from the world of the public library are those people whose mother tongue is not English. There must be provision for those who speak other languages in order that they may retain their cultural heritage. It must be possible for a mother to read stories to her children in her own language whether this be Gujerati, Chinese or Greek. Many libraries are beginning to provide small collections in these minority languages but such services as do exist seem to be very underdeveloped and unsophisticated.(7) It is rare for magazines or records to be provided, and seldom are the prospective users made aware of the services available in a language that they can readily understand.

Moreover, many librarians still apparently do not appreciate the fact that for large numbers of people, particularly those engaged in the service industries, the demands of employment mean unsocial hours or shift work. It would not seem unreasonable, therefore, to enquiry whether librarians have attempted to make provision for such people. What about collections of books in hotel staff rooms or in works canteens for instance? Without doubt such provision would be appreciated.

The mentally disordered, the handicapped and the elderly, are all groups which are easily defined, and once identified easily served. There are no real problems involved apart from those resulting from bureaucracy. However, service to such groups leads on inevitably to thinking of others, less easily defined, and much harder to reach and to serve. What for instance, does one do about the homeless, the unemployed, or the one-parent family? The point to be emphasised is that these groups are not mutually exclusive within any community, and that they all share in the general deprivation that exists. It is hardly surprising that whatever the problem involved, books and reading come a long, long way down the list of priorities.(8) So what is the librarian's role? As one sees it, the librarian can try to provide the compensatory material which will help each individual to surmount his own particular disadvantage, while hoping that in the long term a changing society will remove the disadvantage. It may be that in making such provision as at Highfield, a recreational reading need will become apparent.

It could be that promotion of the 'books are fun' idea is necessary since for many people, as the result of an inadequate or irrelevant education, not only insufficient reading skills but an aversion to learning has meant resistance to the book, as books were consistently 'plugged' in the classroom. Moreover, books are fairly easy to resist or to do without. This does not necessarily mean that people are not reading at all, for even the most run-down of neighbourhoods has its corner shop which sells news-papers, comics, the Fleetway Library Series, and perhaps even a few Ladybird books. Therefore, reading materials are finding their way into every neighbourhood, even if these are often materials of the most basic kind. We must not ignore the significance of this situation. Many people are not averse to the reading of news-papers, comics and novelettes because these in no way resemble the 'books' of the schooldays. In fact, they may even have the added attraction of being liable to confiscation thus giving to the reader a further illicit delight.

In neighbourhoods like this there will always be some parents who recognise the importance of books to the development of their children, and who will attempt to compensate for their own apparent failure to relate to orthodox education by purchasing books. Unfortunately, there is a serious shortage of suitable materials, and were it not for the existence of publications such as the ubiquitous Ladybirds, the task of these parents would be difficult indeed. There are, of course, other parents who do not see the value of books.

However, given that at least some of the people who do not use the public library do possess some kind of a reading instinct, it should be but a short step to providing a service for them. Their resistance to libraries is in fact greater than their resistance to books. If the books - the right books - are made available in an acceptable setting, they will prove to be of use, value and enjoy-ment. Even a mother who is worried about some aspect of her child's health will seek to divert him with a picture book while waiting at the doctor's surgery. A shelf in a corner of the local pub containing some popular paperbacks and appealing informative books on sport, do-it-yourself or welfare rights may attract the regulars. Books should always be seen to be available in this way, a convenient source of both information and pleasure which can be used in almost any location. From the librarian's viewpoint moreover, what better place to provide books than somewhere that people use continuously; the dentist's, the shoe repairer's, the barber's, the launderette, the cafe in the park, or the hospital waiting room? All that is needed is a shelf of inviting books and a sign asking that the books be returned when read. There is no need even for date labels let alone tickets.

The provision of material at those places where the public spend a lot of time needs to span the entire population in terms of age and reading interest. It should be made clear and borne out in practice that those responsible for running centres where books are deposited are *not in any way accountable* for the books. This custodial attitude on the part of librarians has been responsible for alienating many matrons and wardens from using libraries or requesting deposit collections for their centres. As regards the selection of this material it should be self-evident that the bookstock provided ought to be relevant to the particular group of people concerned. Librarians must consider whether they are in fact providing the readers with the kind of material that they, the readers actually want, or instead are supplying books that will be 'good for them' . Can librarians indeed accept the argument that the books that people want are the ones that are good for them? There is a strong argument in favour of exposing people to the kind of material that they might otherwise never encounter, but this has sometimes been used as an excuse to fill the library shelves with some classic non-starters. Let it not be extended to outreach collections. Conversations with the users of outreach collections will very soon disclose a preference for, even a delight in paperback books. One would go so far as to say that outreach simply cannot happen without paperbacks.

The argument over paperbacks is still current in the UK and there remain those librarians who will not buy them. To those who would argue that paperbacks do not last well, one would say that they last well enough. To the argument that is is illegal to bind them - good - for a bound paperback ceases to be a paperback and thus loses its appeal. To the assertion that paperbacks are not worth cataloguing when viewed from the cost-benefit standpoint, one would say that this is an argument against cataloguing, not against the purchase of paper-backs. However, overiding all these in importance is the fact that paperbacks have a strong appeal to almost everyone. They are bright, distinctive and contemporary, unassuming, convenient and, let us admit it, desirable.

One can detect in some librarians the presence of a conservationist attitude whereby books, like the contents of museums, are expected to have a very long life, and, where the care and protection of library materials apparently takes precedence over their use by the public. This attitude must be overcome for it belongs with an academic tradition and has no place in the public library service. There is need of a drastic re-orientation of attitudes, and for a redirection of expertise. Information is required by the public in connection with welfare rights, cash benefits, health services, housing and rent tribunals. This information appears mainly in the form of leaflets, pamphlets, photocopies from newspapers and magazines and so forth. If, information exists to be disseminated, then it ought to be freely available for the widest possible dissemination. The information aspects of librarianship have previously been concerned mainly with academic or scientific enquiry work, and rarely is this of immediate practical help in everyday life. However, librarians must now prepare to do battle on the client's behalf by insisting on acquiring the kind of information that they are most likely to need. All librarians should take advantage of welfare rights courses to make sure that they are well informed on such matters. They should also maintain contact with voluntary organisations who would be able to comment upon test cases and anomalies, recent changes in the law, and benefits.

Having acquired this valuable information, what does the librarian do with it? Stored away in mind or in filing cabinet it is unused, or at least underused. Instead, it should be published and made available to all local information counselling organisations, displayed frequently in local shop windows, used for 'one-off' displays at meetings of action groups, and generally made to work. The librarian who is committed to the spreading of self-help information will appreciate the fact that when such information is required, there is usually somebody in the community to whom an enquirer will go. The people who hold this key position may be doctors, councillors or clergy, or they may have no discernable position, but will perhaps simply be good listeners. They will already have a fund of information in their heads - that is why they are asked - but the librarian can nevertheless play a helpful supporting role in this situation by plying such people with new or revised information. All types of local advice centres and social services departments should be informed of new books or pamphlets relative to their work. Moreover, where possible they should be equipped with this material so that it may be made available for consultation by both their staff and the public. In addition to such publications librarians themselves can contribute through the production of broadsheets and bibliographies on similar themes.

One of the first examples of outreach in Lambeth was the childrens' outdoor storytelling programme which was started in 1966. This has been described in detail elsewhere(9) so suffice to say here that the project developed from the realisation that those children who needed stories most were never to be found in any library. When sought out they were found in parks and play-grounds, in swimming pools and housing estates, and it was to these places that the storytellers went. By now many of these children are well occupied with the activities of newly developed play leadership schemes, at which in addition to other pursuits, books and story sessions are provided by the playleaders. There-fore, the need for storytelling programmes in such places is declining, and it is the isolated child who now occupies our attention. There are children who are confined to the limits of the dingy streets where they live, forbidden to go as far as the park or playground where their peers may be found. These children are now beginning to benefit from occasional visits by a librarian or a para-professional who comes as a friend with a bag full of inviting books and a sympathetic ear.

As with children, so it is with adults. Many are loners, not members of any easily-identified groups. With adults, moreover, there is more likely to be a fear of rejection which often prevents one person from approaching another. This has to be overcome by outreach librarians. Librarians have to be prepared to go to places where they may not be welcome. Lucky indeed is the librarian invited to a claimants' union meeting; he has no right of place there except in the unlikely event of being on benefit himself. To be invited as a guest indicates the existence of a rare trust. Even more difficult to approach are the lone families who do not go to school, or work, do not visit the health clinic or use the social services, never frequent the swimming pool or the park. Short of knocking on doors, which is too much of an intrusion upon privacy, how can they be reached?

The librarian must be prepared to make himself known. He must sit in the pub and chat to the customers; he must run a stall in the market place bodly advertising whatever he thinks will go down well and providing advice when it is needed.(10) He must make the facilities of the library well known to the staff in the employment exchange, social security offices, probation offices and in the offices of his own council's housing, social services and education departments. It is important, however, that all staff are kept informed and not just the directors, managers and organisers. A regular mention in departmental newsletters could help ensure that people will think of contacting the library whenever a problem arises.

The people whom one does manage to contact through direct approach or referral are going to make a variety of demands upon the service. The librarian is never going to be the one to 'cure' poverty, homelessness, or unemployment, but he can be involved in the general campaign against these problems. At the very least he can help alleviate the effects of such evils until a solution is found. The service that he gives will be an intensely personal one. A family with a handicapped child may welcome a handbook which explains the nature of the handicap and its limiting effects, or information about educational or care facilities which will give the family some respite from stress. A man made redundant may be provided with information about re-training facilities so that he may have the opportunity of developing an alternative skill. Whatever the problem if the librarian is able to help once, he can expect to be called upon a second time. For such purposes the librarian must above all be accessible and this aim can best be achieved by his being in some recognisable venue. This could be a storefront centre or more promisingly, a small van which could make random stops at street corners and pub forecourts, and be available to all comers in all weathers. It would be equipped to handle a fair variety of advice/information work, and to provide a small selection of recreational material.

Among the outreach librarian's contacts there may be those in whom an unexploited desire to read for pleasure is discovered. In the kind of library service envisaged, the librarian would begin by providing such materials as seemed likely to be of appeal, gradually encouraging the reader to make use of a nearby 'put-one take-one' collection, located perhaps in a health clinic, bar or local store. However, every convert to books and reading who is won over by the outreach librarian may have to face the fact that he had outgrown the selection he has been weaned on, and that he needs a more comprehensive stock from which to select his reading. If the outreach librarian has done his job well then this reader should be ready to 'take on' the regular public library service.

What ought the public library service be doing in order to attract the new reader? Commercial entertainment and television both cater for the popular imagination through glamorous promotion cleverly advertised. The popular press stirs its public with headlines that are exciting and relevant. The library must also seek to attract users. It should contain a manageable stock with adequate provision of those books and records currently in demand, reflecting pop culture, television and commercial entertainment, sporting personalities and the subjects that everyone is talking about. This type of material should be readily available, and yet it almost certainly is not, without recourse to the reservation system. Childrens' books and adult books should be intermingled and indistinguishable, both to maximise their potential and to avoid embarassing those adults who require simple books. There should of course be newspapers, magazines, records and cassettes, and the library would be freely available for the use of community groups. These groups could include; playgroups, young mothers' clubs, bingo clubs, local societies or political organisations, in fact any group which is in need of this facility. It must be made clear that everyone is welcome rather than merely tolerated.

It is one's personal conviction that libraries comprise the principal barrier to reading so far as a majority of the population is concerned. Libraries are often too big, over-bureaucratic and formal, and their somewhat forbidding image is even today being reinforced by the proliferation of petty rules, fines, registration forms, and the kind of attitude that implies favoured treatment if a book is reserved or renewed. In some places, the public, who after all are only claiming the use of a service for which they pay, are treated to displays of authoritarianism redolent of the atmosphere of the police station. In such surroundings it is an act of daring for one to tamper with the long rows of books all arranged with neat, almost mathematical precision. Consider the contrast one would find upon entering any book-loving home. There the books are unlikely to be as upright and orderly upon the shelves, and this for the simple reason that they are used by the people who own them. It is usually the case moreover, that friends or visitors at the house are unable to resist handling such books. The basic problem for librarians remains the question of how we can encourage library users, let alone non-users, to express their innate hunger for books, and to feel that the books in their local library are community property and are there to be used.

The reader who has been tempted by an outreach librarian into using his local library may be deterred by the time he is two paces inside the door if anything is wrong about the atmosphere of the place. All the work of the outreach librarian will then have come to nought, but even worse, the reader will feel betrayed, and will be twice as hard to win over next time. If we are concerned about putting opportunity in people's way for them to accept or reject as they think fit, it will be the outreach librarian who carries that opportunity to a large part of the population. However, his rate of success is only party dependant upon his own efforts. It is also very heavily dependant upon the back-up library. Let the library make a genuine attempt to be as attractive a place as possible - perhaps aiming to look more like a bookshop than a traditional single-copy library. Let the furniture be so arranged that there are no vast open spaces - a little overcrowding is so much more friendly. Let the library become a real focal point for so many kinds of activities that there is always something going on. In this way there may be a real chance of our holding on to those timid readers so carefully nurtured by the outreach librarian. The outreach librarian can only be as successful as the library will allow.

REFERENCES

1   Nick Moore 'The public library issue decline' *Library Association record* 76, 5, May 1974, 87.
2   Public Libraries and Museums Act 1964.
3   *Liaison* September 1974, 57.
4   National Children's Bureau *Born to fail* 1972.

5 *New society* 25 July 1974. Gordon Pratt's letter on reading need.

6 *Book trolley* 3, 10, June 1973, 3-5.

7 For a pattern of more sophisticated provision in Canada see, Leonard Wertheimer 'New Canadians and the public library: a decade letter' *Unesco bulletin for libraries* XXVIII, 3, May-June 1974, 139-145.

8 W J Martin 'The Highfield community library' *New library world* 75, 893 November 1974, 240-242.

9 Janet Hill *Children are people* London, Hamish Hamilton, 1973.

10 It is not impossible. See Elaine Moss's account of an East End bookstall in *Signal* 15, September 1974, III

OUTREACH IN HAARLEM

MARIE-ANNE HULSHOFF

Social worker attached to the North Holland
County Library Centre, Haarlem

Of all the problems facing public libraries today, few it seems are
more intractable than the continued minority status of the library
service. If use is any guide then, so far as the mass of the public
is concerned, libraries have as yet to prove themselves. It was to
assist in the creation of a relevant library service, one responsive
to the needs of all the people, that the social cultural service of
the North Holland County Library Service was formed. What
follows is an account of the work of this service, which is still the
only one of its kind in Holland. This work has not involved the
staff in large scale projects but, rather, it has consisted of a
careful exploration of what is and is not possible in the quest for
a public library service of widespread and demonstrable utility.

In Holland, County Library Centres have responsibility for the
provision of library services in districts with a population of less
than 30,000 inhabitants. In addition to the general administration
of libraries in the area, they number among their activities, a
library bus service, a school library service, an old peoples' service,
an information service, and, in the case of North Nolland, the
social cultural service. Some forty public libraries are attached to
the North Holland County Library Centre, which set up its social
cultural service at Haarlem in June 1970, aided by a grant from
the Ministry of Culture and Recreation. This grant was converted
to a permanent subsidy in January, 1973, which means that the
social cultural service is now accepted as an integral part of the
public library service. The objects in setting up the service were:
a) to make the library service accessible and attractive to everyone, that is popularising the service and making it more
democratic; b) to give practical assistance to the development
of permanent education.

The author, as a cultural worker attached to the library, was attracted to the idea of working on this project. Together with four students from a nearby social academy she began the process of trying to make contact with the library's public.

It was apparent from the start that, in order to render the services offered by the library both meaningful and attractive, certain obstacles would first have to be removed. Several libraries within the North Holland area were experiencing difficulties owing to the unwelcome presence of young people, mainly teenagers, whose anti-social behaviour was tending to drive other users out of the library. Therefore, as part of the social cultural experiment, meetings were arranged at these libraries, where the problem was discussed directly with the young people concerned. This action was taken not only because there was a major problem for local libraries, but also because there was a problem for the teenagers whose presence the libraries found to be such an embarrassment. The sombre fact was that the young people only frequented the library because there was nowhere else for them to spend their time, no club houses or meeting places where they could go. Therefore, in offering to help these young people, the public library was in fact serving its own best interests, by demonstrating that it had indeed something to offer.

This initial project was followed by an investigation into the part that libraries would play in local society. To this end, informative meetings were organised on topics of local concern, for instance, or redevelopment, high rise/low rise buildings and the like. At these meetings 'information markets' were held whereby local and regional societies, pressure groups, factories and other institutions were each given the opportunity to inform local people about their work. Each of these groups had its own stand, and there was ample opportunity for discussion and the exchange of ideas. Along with these efforts went other programmes aimed at satisfying the library needs of particular groups of people, such as old-age pensioners, children and parents. In the course of the first year, 1970-71, something of the order of 100 meetings were held at five local libraries. The social cultural service initiated these activities and remained in overall supervision, while the planning and execution of the projects took place in cooperation with local librarians and committees.

The staff of the social cultural service were anxious both to gain experience and to test the potential attraction of a dynamic presentation of library service as a means of arousing the enthusiasm of all concerned. Every meeting was built around some central theme, concerning which the local librarian organised an informative exhibition comprised not only of written material but also including posters, transparancies, discs, models and so on. It was possible to borrow this material either during or after the proceedings. The keynote of all these meetings was informality, with the local librarians playing host to the public. Every effort was made to put people at their ease, and there was plenty of opportunity for visitors to meet other people, listen to music, have coffee or browse in the library.

The second year of operation brought certain changes. In the first place, the four students who had been involved in the previous year's activities were replaced by one student and a part-time assistant. In the second place, rather more attention was given to the internal aspects of the operation, with meetings being organised for library staff and members of the library committee. This change in emphasis resulted from an appreciation of the importance of such people to any scheme aimed at providing meaningful library services at the local level. Accordingly, the North Holland Course was devised as a means of making information on topics of local interest available in library circles. It was hoped that through such an approach, librarians working together might discover how their libraries could best participate in these developments. It was at one such meeting that the idea for the creation of 'library work groups' was first mooted. The purpose of these groups was to bring some local knowledge to bear on the proposals emanating from the internal meetings organised by the social cultural service. Hence, the search began for local people with connections in the community, well-versed in community attitudes, possessed of the ability to assess any likely reaction to particular projects, and to foster library/community relations.

Another important innovation during the second year of operation brought changes in the system of selecting programmes for libraries. Whereas in the previous year the determination of such matters had, by and large, been the responsibility of the social cultural service, this was amended in the second year, with individual libraries themselves being free to choose programmes for their own neighbourhood from a central list compiled by the social cultural service. This was done to avoid any possibility of the local librarians having programmes forced upon them from above. It was also in order for librarians to send in suggestions, and to make requests for the kinds of programme that they deemed to be of importance to their locality.

During this second year, 1971-1972, the social cultural service organised a total of fifty nine happenings or activities, of which twenty six were internal, that is aimed at library staff or officials, and thirty three external, designed for readers. These activities took place in twelve public libraries. The programmes were linked with a series of informative exhibitions which it was customary to hold in local public libraries. These affairs ran for a six-week period, and the intention was to bring a special topic or theme to the public notice. These 'special theme' exhibitions were compiled at a central point for subsequent distribution to various local libraries. Prior to this, meetings were held with local librarians at which material for inclusion could be discussed, and any necessary arrangements made either for orders or for the reorganisation of local library stocks to facilitate the projects. The library publicity department was responsible for the visual layout and presentation of each exhibition.

The information service prepared indexes and bibliographies on the topics concerned, with both print and non-print materials being listed. The public was able to borrow any of this material on request. The planning and execution of these 'special theme' exhibitions made considerable demands on all concerned, and the social cultural service both instigated the programmes and co-ordinated the proceedings. As a 'follow up' to these exhibitions, programmes were organised at local libraries covering such topics as town and country planning, diet, education and society. As far as was possible, local organisations such as schools and parent teacher committees were involved in the running of these activities. In addition, the social cultural service offered local librarians a choice of programmes designed to attract special groups of library users, for instance, musical programmes for young people or for the top class of the primary school. There was even a programme in which, with the help of material from the library, children could make their own books.

In the third year, the pattern of work of the social cultural service changed again, with the decision to amalgamate its external and internal activities. Moreover, in this year it was decided to concentrate upon working with four types of organisations:- the churches, the trades unions, those organisations engaged in work with old people, and the county and local authorities. Thereafter, internal meetings were arranged in collaboration with those county or regional organisations having local branches. At these meetings, representatives of the organisations concerned talked about their work to librarians and committee members, and indicated what they expected from libraries in the way of co-operation and assistance. This, therefore, enabled the library service and a section of its public to come together to plan the basis of their future working relationship, a partnership founded on mutual understanding of their respective roles in society.

That this was a genuine working partnership was shown by the manner in which these outside organisations adjusted their oper-ations to the needs of the library alliance. Increasingly, the iniative in such matters came from outside the library as the organisations began to realise the value to them of a good library service. Soon not only enquiries and requests for assistance came flooding into the libraries, but also, suggested themes for the regular six-weekly exhibitions. Moreover, the meetings between both sides, that is the libraries and the various organisations, although taking place inside the local libraries were, nevertheless, held under joint auspices. Thus, whether the subject under dis-cussion concerned ecumenism or the needs of old people, under such circumstances it was possible, on the one hand to build up a coordinated course of action, and on the other, to meet the special needs of the local situation in the implementation of combined projects. It was the consideration of local needs that prompted the idea for library 'work groups', and these groups although mooted a year before, actually came into being in the third year of the project. They appear to be living up to the expectations of those who felt that with the aid of such groups, local society could be made more aware of the untapped potential of the library service.

All in all, the social cultural service organised thirty nine activities on the course of the third working year of the project, fourteen of which were internal and twenty five external. These took place in eleven different public libraries. The personnel involved were the same as in the previous year, that is one part-time assistant and a student from a social academy.

We are now in the fourth year of operation of the social cultural service. In a survey of the internal meetings of the 1972-1973 session, it was found that the evening spent with the county and local authorities was the one most appreciated by the librarians. In attendance at this meeting were the Clerk of the County Council of North Holland, the head of the information department, and representatives of the local council. In the informal setting of the meeting it was possible for people to get to know one another, and for the librarians present to set up appointments with their council secretary, information official or clerk for social affairs, in order that problems might be worked out at the local level. As to the overall programme of meetings, both local librarians and the county library centre were agreed on the wisdom of continuing with the type of project whereby, through close liason with other organisations, libraries could aim their services at groups with whom these organisations maintained contact.

In this present year of operation, the service has returned with renewed vigour to an aspect of its work first embarked on when it began in 1970. Then, as now, librarians were conscious of the unsatisfactory relationship that obtained between young people in the fourteen to eighteen year old group and the public library. The problem still remains as to how any librarian, however well-intentioned, can seriously hope to attract young people to an institution whose sole attraction is apparently its usefulness as a meeting place. Indeed, rather more is involved here than a simple shortage of relevant material, because at the heart of this question is a basic problem of communication. In order to resolve the difficulties created by the presence of unruly young people in certain libraries, librarians, must first learn to communicate with these youngsters, and then attempt to persuade them that the library service does indeed have something for everyone.

Given the nature of the task and the size of the group involved secondary school children, lower trade school children, and young people at work - it was decided to narrow the field some-what and concentrate the effort on the two latter groupings, lower trade school children and young people already at work. It was felt that the problem was greatest amongst these young people because, neither their home nor their school background directed them much towards reading. Moreover, for those already in a working situation there was little to suggest any likely conversion to the reading habit. Following the success of previous programmes, it was agreed that the familiar, well-tried method of direct contact with all interested parties would be employed from the outset. Nevertheless, the staff fully realised the very real problems connected with this particular project, and understood that if anything were to come of it, it would take a very long time. Moreover, we realised that it is not the job of librarians to teach others to read, and that to attempt this would be to exceed our professional authority. Therefore, as in previous years, contact was made with other organisations, for instance, lower trade schools, and education centres for young working people. Guidance was also sought from two other bodies, the Critical Debating Centre, and the Anne Frank Organisation in Amsterdam, both of which operate in the lower trade educational area and in factories.

This project involves considerable collaboration between all concerned and its 'modus operandi' was laid down in consultation between students from educational centres for young working people and two regional educational authorities. These education authorities wrote to the schools in their areas suggesting that they join in the project. In addition, advertisements urging people to participate were placed in educational papers, and, by means of a pamphlet sent to all schools, teachers were also invited to help. Cooperation was also forthcoming from the educational inspector, who readily acceded to a request that teachers wishing to do so would have two days free to participate in the project. Almost one hundred people accepted the invitation; some seventy of whom came from twenty five libraries in the public library sector, fourteen from the lower trade schools, and eleven from some six education centres for young working people.

Meetings were convened to discuss the question of how schools, educational centres and public libraries could cooperate and work together for the benefit of young people, if not today then for the youngsters of the future. Four evening and two daytime meetings were held, and for the evening sessions North Holland was divided into four regions, as otherwise the groups would have been over large, and the participants would have had to travel too far in order to attend. Nevertheless, the meetings still made considerable demands on the time and energy of all those taking part. At the first evening meeting, various people arrived expecting to find that the library had a ready made solution to the problem. On learning that such was hardly the case, some of them immediately withdrew from the proceedings. On the second evening, an attempt was made to obtain insights into each other's work and, to this end, the separate organisations concerned each supplied information about themselves. The room rang with the sound of voices. On the third evening, an effort was made to find out what it is that young working people actually do for both recreation and information. As a direct result, many schools in the area decided, on their own initiative to launch surveys into the reading habits of their pupils. We had ourselves considered the central preparation of a questionaire about reading habits, but had been reluctant to give still more work to the participants from the schools and the educational centres. On reflection, an organised survey would undoubtedly have given better results. Such a survey, if sufficiently detailed and thorough would be the best means of penetrating the difficulties which obtain from a lack of data.

In any case, discussions with school teachers and with workers from educational centres, resulted in the following disclosures:-

Many families from the groups being interviewed possess very few books.

In more cases than we had expected, even a newspaper is missing.

In the newspapers, people primarily read the articles about crime, court hearings and accidents.

Where there is a women's magazine in the house, boys tend to read that as well as girls. This could signify that, where understandable reading matter is available, this will be read even if it is directed towards another group.

Bookstall reading matter and paperbacks are very popular among working people.

Information such as, for instance, that which is contained in publications issued by the trade unions, only gets through to a certain proportion of these young people, that is the ones who have had better opportunities.

It is also more than clear that the public library, so far as practically this entire group, and even some of the teachers, are concerned, is an institution that lies completely beyond the sphere of their day-to-day and working lives.

These evening meetings were followed by daytime ones at which plans were made for enabling groups of young working people to gain some understanding of the potential of the library service. Furthermore, libraries in places where the schools had not participated in the project took steps to awaken interest in the scheme at these schools. At the same time, study groups were formed around certain problems which had risen during the course of the evening meetings. These covered the following subjects:- manpower, presentation, acquisition and processing.

Moreover, after the daytime meetings, we started to implement specific local projects with young people. As of now this is going on in some eleven libraries, each of which had chosen a largely different approach. In one instance, the librarian has first become acquainted with the school or education centre by attending lessons given there; in another, he has begun by playing host to teachers at the public library. In another case, the librarian has started by bringing a group to the library and familiarising it with the system by means of, say, a treasure hunt. Yet another has confronted the young people with the library material by letting them compile a woman's magazine.

The reader will probably be surprised to learn that these local collaboration groups have come into being, given that the difficulties involved in getting young people to come to libraries, and in enabling them to benefit from libraries, are fundamental and structural. The fact is that they have been brought into being and are still working, and this for two reasons. Firstly, because the people taking part believe that one can really get to know a problem by tackling it, and that one can only conquer it by learning the hard facts about it through experience. Secondly, because even if the final target is unattainable this still does not prevent small improvements from being made in the short term.

In the course of the work a number of problems begin to show themselves very clearly. In the first place, it seems that far too much printed matter is based upon the language used by the middle-class. From what information is available, it seems that hardly any consideration is given to the language of other groups. It is hoped that the problem of 'comprehensability' is high on the list of priorities of the scientific and training insitutes. This applies not only to recreative literature but also to informative literature. It is also to be hoped that all those organisations that have anything to do with the needs of the 'man in the street' will occupy themselves to a considerable extent with the provision of literature that is readable and understandable for everyone. One would consider publishers to be among such organisations. Moreover, it is one of the responsibilities of the public libraries, and of the educational training centres and lower trade schools, to continue to stress that a great need still exists in this respect. Furthermore, it has been assumed here that 'printed sources' will for the immediate future continue to play a major role in the imparting of information. This may be a debatable point but this is hardly the place to debate it.

In the second place, it is a fact that most librarians have been trained to give service to a social group markedly different from the one at present under consideration; to people already familiar with the written word. Moreover very few in library circles know much about working with such groups, and many librarians would admit to being at a disadvantage in this respect. In the course of this project a definite demand has arisen for 'additional training' on this point. The social cultural service, in conjunction with local librarians, is now operating an 'in-service training programme', which gives priority to these aspects. A long-term solution would be the inclusion of these aspects as part of the normal education of all librarians.

A third problem is that the operation and organisation of the public library is still almost completely based on the needs of users of the library. A reconsideration of the aims of the public library and thereby, the role of the librarian has not yet been successfully accomplished. Because of this, new developments are often too closely bound up with particular people. Hence, a good working enterprise, built up perhaps after great difficulty in finding space and money, can collapse if even one assistant should leave. This is equally true of the work of educational centres and lower trade schools and therefore, collective experiments ought to be included in the working programmes of all such organisations.

Finally, there is the problem of manpower, and the fact that librarians rarely have sufficient time for even existing library users. There have been complaints about this from libraries as well as from the general public. Imagine what the position would be were we to succeed in attracting large numbers of new readers into the library; readers who, moreover, would be likely to require more guidance than does the present reading public? This problem is simply a question of money; simple that is, compared with the previously mentioned, much more complicated structural problems. A solution to this problem could come about simply through the granting of sufficient money by the authorities. However, it is hardly likely that the government will be able to satisfy all demands at the same time, such as provision of a complete service to existing users, and the orientation of the library towards new readers.

Therefore, for the time being, we must cope with the situation by such means as are available; hopefully with a little extra help from the authorities. This means that libraries must seriously reflect upon the priorities in their work. Of all the things that could be so labelled, one only has been chosen here, and that is the choice of the library's main target group within the community. On this point there can be no hesitation. To begin with, the County Library Centre Haarlem, already made a choice when in 1970 it set up the social cultural service. Secondly, this kind of choice must be made because, 'The library can, and may not, neglect the community development process. It should not neglect the striving towards a greater democracy and a more critical outlook on life, a greater justice in worldwide perspective and the realisation of the "education permanente". The library can, and may not pass by, but must even become involved itself. The public library must become a more democratic institution in respect of and for everyone. The library has the duty to project itself more, in particular to those groups for whom the library could be most useful'.(1)

These sentiments were completely supported in the contents of a Dutch Government statement issued during a parliamentary debate on the subject of library law, in Janury, 1974. The entire statement enlarges on the principle that a serious attempt must be made to give to everyone the opportunity of becoming a 'complete member of society'. All available means should be employed to this end - radio, television, education, training and development work, but also the resources of public libraries. This means that the greatest pressure must be exerted where the need is greatest, that is in backward situations, and while there is still a chance to do something about it. One group which, with this object in view, is still capable of being reached, is that at which our project is directed, namely the young working peoples' group or the young working peoples' group of the future.

The concept embodied in the law is still very much words on a page. The reader must view our collaboration project as a bold, yet modest, effort by librarians, education centre workers, and teachers to prevent its remaining confined to paper. It is an attempt to translate theory into practice. These experiments must be continued and, indeed, applied on a much larger scale, for only by such means can service-orientated provision grow up to become an integral part of library work. The working environment must, however, be improved. In the first place, the government should provide effective opportunities by setting up the necessary machinery. In the second place, all levels of workers both inside and outside the library, must be made aware of those priorities so essential if projects for the disadvantaged are to have any chance of success.

REFERENCES
1   D Raumer *On the way to a new public library.* A speech at the opening of the North Holland Social Cultural Service, Haarlem, 1970)

LIBRARIES AND LITERACY IN GREAT BRITAIN

MARGARET REDFERN

Senior Lecturer, Department of Librarianship,
The Polytechnic of North London

What percentage of the adult population of the world cannot read or write? As librarians we can find an answer to that question, we can also identify sources that define functional literacy, that indicate the nature of reading problems, that debate the value of literacy.

What percentage of the adult population of Great Britain cannot read? As librarians we can examine the published statements and find a somewhat blurred outline of a seemingly grim picture. Studies in reading standards in schools indicate that postwar improvements have stopped and there is now cause for concern.(1) Add to that the estimate of two million adult illiterates quoted in the campaign document of the British Association of Settlements, 'A right to read'(2) and the picture becomes a little clearer.

A basic assumption is net that reading has any intrinsic value. rather that it is a life coping skill in our industrialised society and as such it is the right of each individual to acquire and develop it. If formal education cannot help people to acquire and develop such skills then society must provide some further support. The debates about functional literacy, reading ages, reading readiness, interpretation, comprehension, are well documented in educational and sociological literature. The fact of the matter is that at the present time there are many people who have passed the school leaving age who do not have the ability to decode graphic symbols and to reconstruct some sort of meaning from them. These people are handicapped as surely as if they were lacking a limb; partially sighted; socially inadequate; suffering from muscular wastage or institutionalised.

One can identify the reasons that reading skills are not developed by some people during schooling, there are the individual based reasons such as bad sight, deafness, dyslexia, emotional disturbance; and the environment based reasons such as lack of schooling, changes of schooling, unstable home, bad teaching. Each profile of an adult who cannot read reveals another combination of factors that could be the cause of that particular person's problem. It is important to note that there is a distinction to be drawn between the essentially language problem of the immigrant who has not yet acquired a command of English and the lack of reading skill of the indigenous population. The position of the adult illiterate is difficult to appreciate if from the age of seven one has rapidly decoded a lifetime of messages. There is a temptation to assume that it might feel like travelling in a foreign country - if only it did - and the illiterate knew that the shame and isolation would end in a fortnight's time. Unfortunately for many who reach adult years unable to read, the efforts involved in learning may quite defeat them. For others the efforts are possible, if they have the care of another individual and are supported by techniques/equipment and materials geared to their own particular needs.

For years there have been dedicated people working to alleviate the problem by tuition of adult non-readers, there is a long history of work with adults, in remand homes and prisons and small-scale schemes in deprived urban communities. In the last decade various organisations have claimed public money and support for more formalised tuition schemes. Two well known university settlements working in the field are Liverpool, and Cambridge House in London. The work of the settlements in the community has an honorable tradition of social conscience working in a practical way. The Cambridge House Literacy scheme began in 1965 with some local teenagers who requested help with their reading and writing. The Inner London Education Authority and some charitable trusts have supported the scheme since 1967. The work in London has developed fairly quickly, perhaps not as quickly as the organisers would wish. It is based on one-to-one tuition, (the 'each one teach one' principle of Laubach fame) by volunteer tutors drawn from all age groups. The scheme handles some 500 to 600 students out of an estimated 100,000 people who need help in the Greater London area. The Liverpool university settlement adult literacy project was inaugurated in 1971 in consultation with local and central government departments and voluntary organisations. It aims to provide individual and small group tuition for some 200 out of the estimated 14,000 who may need help. Both schemes indicate that seventy five percent of the students are men: both schemes rely on volunteers who are not necessarily teachers who, therefore, need training sessions and an efficient back-up system such as meetings with other tutors, information bulletins, and collection of materials.

There have been many other projects at local level operating through a variety of sponsors. In Manchester, a literacy project was started in 1968 by the Council of Social Services Volunteer Bureau at the suggestion of the Family Service Unit. An urban aid grant allowed organisers to be appointed and the scheme extended to Salford and Stockport in 1971. 'The need is far greater than generally supposed', states the foreword to a hand-book describing the scheme.(3) For reasons of space it is not possible to list schemes exhaustively here, but it should be noted that action on adult illiteracy has been under-taken by a range of institutions and individuals. Colleges of education, colleges of technology, adult evening institutes, remedial teachers, education psychologists, formal volunteer groups, as well as voluntary efforts on the part of individuals have all been involved in the fight against illiteracy. This brief list suggests that there might be problems for any national coordination body in terms of disseminating information about methods and materials. There can be no doubt that the emergence of the United Kingdom Reading Association and the great deal of interest in and study of, reading, by institutes of education and the National Foundation of Educational Research have alerted the country to some of the current problems relating to the development of reading skills.

It is difficult to pinpoint when the concern for adult illiterates began to register with more people than just the organisers of local tuition schemes up and down the country. The evidence as to whether the rate of adult illiteracy is higher now than it was thirty years ago is slight, what is established is the present degree of concern. The development of the campaign by the British Association of Settlements produced hard evidence of interest, in the response they received to various one-day workshops on the theme of adult illiteracy in 1973/74. The policy document pushed the idea forward, and the setting up of a committee under the chairmanship of Lady Plowden the level of concern. In fact, the government made a grant of one million pounds available in 1974 to be administered by the National Institute for Adult Education. This once only payment may not measure up to the scale of the problem, but it must be seen as a contribution towards the development of the proper resources to fight illiteracy in adults. Only one-half percent of the people in need of help are receiving it, and forty-eight percent of education authorities are not making any provisions.(4)

In referring to the scale of the problem it becomes important to keep a perspective on what is a highly emotional and appealing crusade. Discussing the social problems of the illiterate at the Library Association in London during April 1974, Peter Clyne, author of *The disadvantaged adult* Longmans, 1973, argued that we should question the wisdom of imposing 'our' skill as it may be of dubious value to both individuals and to society as a whole. Literacy may break the sequence of deprivation but it is not the only link to be reforged. In creating higher expectations society may be creating ugly problems for the individuals who have learnt to read, as well as for their families and for the community. Not unexpectedly, this view was rejected by the audience of teachers and librarians. Nevertheless, there is a serious point to consider, exactly what is it hoped to achieve? Bringing boots and bibles to the poor is not appropriate in the 1970's, if it ever was, but it should be clear that functional literacy for everyman could allow a healthier society to emerge. There is a long way to go before the political impact of a totally literate society in the terms of the gentleman scholar is likely to be felt! It is important to stress the value of reading as a survival skill for here and now, a skill which can develop when practised. Librarians hold a highly responsible position here to ensure that every encouragement is given to individuals to practice such skills. This of course, implies that there will be appropriate materials available.

Somewhat reluctantly, in the absence of any other framework, the London based scheme has been used as something of a prototype. It is of interest to note that other schemes, and libraries, are using the Cambridge House list of commercially produced materials as a basic selection tool. It is hoped that as more experience is gained and more money made available, that some detailed evaluative work will be done on reading materials for the adult non-reader. One of the most serious problems connected with the teaching of adult illiterates is the total lack of suitable material. The American experience foundered time and time again on this point. All too frequently materials are inappropriate both in vocabulary and content.(5)

In Great Britain, people working with adults in order to develop reading skills have no choice but to create material of their own, often based on magazine cuttings and personal flair, or to rely on the series commerically produced for slow or reluctant readers of younger age groups. There has been a concentration on the teenage end of the market, fairly obviously there is a demand at that level since the output from the schools in the last decade has included high numbers of young adults with reading problems. The materials on the market often exhibit the worst signs of a society composed of 'haves' and 'havenots'. Many include contrived family situations, totally incredible characters whose language is stilted and whose behaviour is dull. This perhaps is not the place to debate the problem of restricted language and social class, but it is arguably true that for many adults who have a range of feelings and skills other than reading, material geared to the adolescent will seem patronising. Perhaps what is even more important is that it will not encourage and sustain effort to master the new skill. There is an urgent need for material that appeals to adults and to things that motivate them. This will often be utilitarian and practical in aspect, although it must also be noted that fantasy and horror often capture the interest of a reluctant reader. Adults relate strongly to subject areas, job situations, community problems, self-improvement. Those stuffy labels mask the meaning. It is absolutely vital to demonstrate the value of the skill in terms that the adult can appreciate. Instructions on household appliances, clothing or packaging have an immediate relevance, as does the highway code and street signs to someone who wants to learn to drive. There have been so many descriptions now of the problems of an illiterate that perhaps these points ought not to be laboured further. One would merely add one's personal view that this urgent need for material can best be met by people with experience and understanding of the teaching of adults. Such people are most likely to be able to determine an appropriate level and content. Of course, the problem is aggravated by the need for publishers to know the market and to assess financial returns. While thousands of people are made to feel embarrassed and frustrated in their sense of failure through a lack of reading ability, this in itself is hardly proof of market potential. It is to be hoped that the current campaigns both against literacy itself and the social stigma it brings, will provide some 'spin-off' in the shape of genuine figures of illiteracy. These can be used to establish the need for new materials.

The three year project devised by the BBC to help to reduce the extent of adult illiteracy will necessarily go part way towards solving the problem of materials. The television programmes are due to start in Autumn 1975 whilst some radio sessions may start earlier in the year. Fortunately the BBC do not see their programmes as the only source of information or instruction and they are anxious to refer students to local schemes. Since it is appreciated that learning to read may start from zero level, the programmes will start at that point and work to a reading age of seven plus. There is the assumption that other agencies can support students at that level of attainment. Naturally such programmes will generate some printed materials; although the first questions to be asked are fairly daunting, how does one design material which a totally illiterate adult can use on his own without help, how does one get the items to the student? Printed materials for the tutors are also planned. The possible effect of such provision through the national network of television could be very exciting. The programmes could help more people to understand the problems, to encourage and sustain the learning of relatives or friends who might need help, and generally serve to lift the taboos of being illiterate.

The justification for the involvement of libraries in any plans to combat illiteracy seems so obvious that one risks banality. One also risks accusations of missionary zeal and imposition of middle class values until drawn up short by the only mandate for survival in professional practice, which is library legislation. The normal parliamentary language allows that a comprehensive and efficient service be provided to all persons desiring to use it. This allows a great deal, or very little in the way of service to the individuals in the community. It does not seem perverse to suggest that adult illiterates should receive some attention from libraries for as yet they have no means of judging whether they are desirous of using the services. If we support activities to increase and promote reading skills in the population we support ourselves in some measure. Such a pragmatic approach has little appeal but should not be ignored?

Library response to the problems of illiteracy can operate at two levels. One level is based on the point that at the present time the most significant activity of the public library (in the eyes of the public at least) is book lending; there is no denying our honorable tradition of book provision. The fashionable view that print is outmoded, the book in decline, may allow the librarian to calm his fears about the provision of cassettes, films, tapes, video recordings, prints etc. Nevertheless it seems unlikely that railway timetables, social security procedures, motor cycle manuals will be on instruction tape/slide presentations in the foreseeable future. This might suggest that the librarian can accept a degree of print domination of the stock for some time. Surely it then makes sense to encourage all members of the community to use that stock. Ironically in the case of encouraging the new reader the librarian must consider many printed materials that are not in the conventional book form, eg, word games, reading kits and pamphlet issues.

The other level of concern is the duty to consider minority groups and their needs while maintaining the comprehensive service. Such groups may be opera lovers, biologists or the socially deprived. Much of the professional literature stresses that the public library serves the individual and stress is put on the assessment of the service by the individual. This is interesting because so often the ability or willingness of the institution to respond to the needs of an individual is strictly limited.

Fortunately, theory and practice in the area of provision for the adult illiterate and their tutors could well move closer together if some of the best of the current library practices are more widely adopted. At the moment, public library involvement with literacy schemes is rather limited. Since the schemes are administered by a diversity of interests, as mentioned previously, it is hardly surprising that librarians may feel confused as to their potential role. Added to which it is predictable that within any professional body there will be disagreement about what constitutes professional behaviour. So it is with librarians, some are on record as denying the matter of concern, others dispute the existence of illiterates in the area, and many consider that they should wait until demand is manifest. Others, thankfully, are committed to doing all they can to support the work with potential new readers.

Such support ranges from the provision of extra copies of slow learning texts in the junior library, to the more positive collection of a variety of materials. These can include word games, wall charts, pamphlets, and the more common readers retained for the use of tutors and students, all available with sympathetic guidance from an informed member of staff. There are examples of librarians publishing articles in the local press in order to open the discussion on illiteracy.(6) There are attempts to integrate the community-based services of tutors, educationalists, and librarians by the use of local radio. Staffordshire was the first library system to try the idea of making remedial tapes available in public libraries, naturally in the privacy of study carrels. Many libraries already offer halls, meeting rooms, or the library itself after hours, as accommodation for literacy counselling, teaching or the merely administrative meetings of voluntary tutors and organisers. There is really no reason why this could not become accepted practice throughout the country. The library is well placed with its neighbourhood-based buildings and, moreover, it forms a fairly neutral ground for both students and tutors, lacking as it does quite the stigma of school, and being without the distractions of teaching in a home. Already many librarians have taken the logical step beyond this point, opening their premises after hours so that teaching may take place, or that small groups of people developing the reading habit can visit the library, look at a range of books and magazines, and learn a little more about overcoming the barriers to library use. These barriers are familiar, and sometimes forgotten, hence they merit repetition. The language used in library procedures can sound like another skill to be learned and many act as a barrier. The building itself may be oppressive, as may be the arrangement and layout of the stock, the classification scheme, the atmosphere, the condition of the books and, dare one say it, the staff. All of these can be overcome some of the time and some of them all of the time. For adult readers new to the library it is crucial that every effort be made to overcome the barriers, and that support be offered in the venture into our world. The idea ? To encourage them to stay in it. Learning to read is after all only a beginning.

Librarians in Britain have been adamant in declaring the

inappropriateness of their attempting themselves to teach adult illiterates or to develop reading improvement programmes as has been done in the United States. This is a view with which one finds it difficult to disagree. Regretably, having taken this decision, many leave the matter altogether and await articulated demands on the service before considering provision for this group of the disadvantaged. It comes as a shock to realise that many educated but disabled people have difficulties in establishing their rights and ensuring that these are freely offered by society. Battles have been fought by vocal, secure members of communities in order to improve the provision of library facilities for the disabled. How much more difficult is it likely to be for the less vocal, less secure?

If the national campaign and television project succeed, in the next three to five years we could find a time when people will come forward in great numbers seeking help. This will be for tuition at the very elementary stage, and at what one might term the new reader stage. If librarians are not ready for this they will have failed in their professional duty to consider the future needs of the community. A quote that seems appropriate here both because of the content and the date is from *Literacy activities in public libraries* USA, 1966 (7). In other words, *eight years ago* this comment was made. ' "When they become readers we will serve them". If we wait that long and it will seem like tomorrow, we will not have contributed to the very real national effort which is going on right now. Other educational agencies will know it, but worse than that, the former illiterate will know it. He will know and respond accordingly.' There is a need for the librarian to build up the expectations in his area of service that the libraries can and will provide space, materials and guidance in connection with developing reading skills. This means action now. Action to consult with all interested groups in the community, liaison with development councils, adult education advisors, councils for voluntary service, remedial teachers. Action to alert staff, to the size and nature of the problem and their concern in the matter; this is a classic case where a policy statement or official memo will not cover the management responsibility; it calls for information, instruction and encouragement to maintain a high degree of responsiveness to each individual seeking help. Action to select, maintain and exploit appropriate materials, some of which will not be in traditional forms and will need more flexible approaches to acquisition, control and storage as compared to the normal range of books and recorded materials. Action to disseminate information as widely as possible about what the library does and could do to help tutors and students, the information is useless if merely stored on a poster, in a file or in someone's head.

Such actions are all within the normal responsibilities of managing a library service for the public, there is nothing revolutionary about them. It would not even be revolutionary to suggest that staff be appointed as reading advisors. There is already a social services librarian in post in Cornwall County and a reading advisor at Birmingham. Of course financial stringency works against the creation of many new positions but surely the services of metropolitan districts must consider the needs of this case very seriously, there have been literacy provisions in the major urban centres for years which indicates the size of the problem. From the number of librarians known to be active as volunteer tutors there is no doubt that there is a wealth of interest and experience in libraries that could be tapped to develop services. The nature of the adult problem suggests that it is insensitive to allocate a children's librarian as an advisor (paradoxically as many have a developed knowledge about learning reading skills) the adult need is somewhat different. Perhaps this is another area where efforts to overcome library produced barriers is indicated? There is a desparate need for adult lending/reference staff to work more closely with colleagues in the children's libraries. It seems that many volunteer tutors on library staffs do not think to discuss this activity with their colleagues, a reflection of the general library tendency to undersell themselves? It is this factor which is largely to blame for the low expectations about the library service generally.

There must be many reasons why the libraries were not consulted in the preliminary planning stages of the national campaign or the BBC project. One inescapable fact is that they were not considered significant in such planning. The important point is to ensure that more and more libraries are seen to play a part in attempts to increase reading competence. When the million pound grant is spent why not house some collections of materials, or technical equipment, such as video recorders to film television output, in libraries? Perhaps then all the highly impressive professional statements on cultural centres, value and use to the community, outreach, role of the library could stop echoing in space, and could be demonstrated as facts by the 1980's. Perhaps then public libraries would be filled by people of all sorts and conditions actually using the storehouse of knowledge that we work so hard to maintain.

REFERENCES

1   K B Start and B K Wells *The trend of reading standards* London, NFER, 1972.

2   British Association of Settlements *A right to read* London, BAS, 1972.

3   Robert Roberts *Teaching adult illiterates* Manchester, Manchester/Salford Council of Social Service, 1972.

4   Jane Mace 'Can you read this article?' In, *Morning star* 29 October, 1974, 4.

5   Helen Lyman *Library materials in service to the new adult reader* Chicago, American Library Association, 1973.

6   M W Devereux 'The writing on the wall' In, *Salford civic news* Autumn, 1974.

7   Bernice Macdonald *Literacy activities in public libraries* Chicago, American Library Association, 1966, 35.

LIBRARY SERVICES TO INDIAN AND PAKISTANI IMMIGRANTS IN GREAT BRITAIN

S K CROKER

Library Assistant, BBC FILM and VT Library

This chapter had its genesis in a survey which the author helped to carry out during 1971,(1) and although there has been considerable change since that date one would think that the observations based upon the survey are still reasonably valid. When a group of immigrants settle in a particular country, they immediately present both the local community and the country with certain educational, linguistic, social, moral, cultural and historical problems. Often there are prejudices for them to overcome, as well as problems connected with housing, employment and education. They can place great strain upon aspects of the country's administrative system, for example, the social welfare system, and this alone does not help their status in that country. Some immigrants bring additional problems with them in that they want to keep close ties (of language and culture) with their own country; others wish to break these ties and adapt completely to their new country's way of life.

The United Kingdom having once been the centre of a vast empire has been and still is prone to large scale immigration. The largest of these immigrant groupings have all been white, with the Irish, Canadians and Australians leading the table of arrivals. It is, however, the fourth and fifth largest immigrant groups whose coming has created the most comment, the immigrants from Asia. In 1970, some 65,815 Indian immigrants entered the country, and 43,139 Pakistanis. Altogether there are about 360,000 Asian immigrants in the United Kingdom, although this is only a rough estimate as few authorities agree on these figures. These Asians have settled all over Great Britain, many coming to join members of their family who had been earlier arrivals in search of work. The main areas of settlement have tended to be in industrial regions, for example, in Birmingham, Coventry, Walsall and

Wolverhampton, Glasgow, Huddersfield, Bradford, Nottingham and the London Borough of Ealing.

Very little accurate information is available concerning the size of the Asian communites and the extent to which they make use of libraries. Indeed, even such basic information as language needs is not always clear, and often comes to light only after specific efforts have been made. It is probable that only a small proportion of the newcomers is interested in using libraries, and in the main this would tend to be the public library, or, if they are young enough, the school library. Library provision for immigrants is something of comparatively recent vintage, becoming established during the mid-1960's, yet in those areas where librarians have taken the initiative in building up contacts it is clear that the number of immigrants using the library is increasing all the time.

In spite of the problems that ethnic minority groups cause librarians, there are signs of a growing interest in meeting their needs, and a greater willingness to explore more flexible and innovative approaches. Libraries do have a positive contribution to make, not only to the educational and cultural welfare of the newcomers, but also in the promotion of understanding between such groups and indigenous populations. However, before the library can help these people, something must be known of their language and culture, of what makes them 'tick'.

Many immigrants do speak English, but the provision of books in their mother tongue is appreciated by them, and the demand still outstrips the supply. Moreover, apart from the fact that many newcomers will never acquire a good working knowledge of English, there will always remain that smaller group of professional people, conversant in two or more languages, and keen to keep abreast of literary developments not only in their new country but also in their country of origin. This is an important factor in their personal development, and one which the library can aid. Moreover, some libraries have benefited greatly from the knowledge of such people through assistance in the areas of book selection, cataloguing and the listing on new acquisitions. News about the library has spread quickly where such contacts have been fostered, and few other promotional ideas have proved to be necessary.

120

Most of the Asians belong to one or other of the cultural or religious organisations which exist in great numbers. Some of these have their own small collection of books, for example at Gravesend and at Bradford, where there are small libraries at local Sikh temples. A somewhat larger collection of Hindi materials is now located at the Indian High Commission in London, and it is a valuable supplementary source for librarians interested in Hindi works. Until 1967, libraries relied upon the holdings of the India Office Library for Indian and Pakistani books. This research library in fact served as a circulating collection until in March 1967, provision was stopped to all libraries except those in prisons and hospitals. In fact, the service previously offered had very little relation to the book needs of the immigrant communities, and furthermore, the time involved in dispatching books had begun to encroach upon the staff time of the India Office librarians.

As a result of the decision to end the India Office service, many libraries had to face the problem of whether or not to provide their own local collections of Asian materials. A dichotomy arose here between those libraries that were prepared to supply these materials, and to tackle such problems as selection and acquisition, and those where it was felt that in order to encourage integration, no books in Asians languages ought to be provided. At the end of 1967, about thirty library authorities had started collections; by 1971/72 some forty authorities had done so.

A grant from the Community Relations Commission of £2,000 enabled an Asian Central Circulating Library to be established at Birmingham Public Library. This collection has about 4,500 books, and all in all some thirty five other libraries subscribe to the service. The costs of staff are met by Birmingham Public Library, and subscription costs are £30 per year, which entitles members to loans of 100 books which can be changed up to three times annually. This collection is particularly useful to those libraries which are finding provision difficult or uneconomic.

Despite the existence of the Birmingham scheme, other libraries having large Asian settlements within their catchment areas have developed their own collections. Thus, Wolverhampton Public Library has about 2,000 volumes; 1,000 in Hindi and 1,000 in Urdu and Punjabi. It also has about fifty Asian gramophone records, a large number of 'Teach Yourself English' records, and

121

a selection of Asian newspapers and periodicals. At West Bromwich there are about 1,000 books in Hindi, Urdu and Punjabi, while Coventry has nearly the same. Bradford has a growing collection of Urdu materials, while the London Borough of Ealing has 2,500 volumes at its Southall Library covering the five main languages, especially Punjabi. In overall terms, it is the Midlands which is the area of greatest demand for Indian and Pakistani language books, and it is there where the greatest level of provision is to be found.

When the Asians first made their presence felt upon the library, little in the way of book selection was possible or, indeed, attempted. Librarians faced with demands for books in various Indian languages were heavily dependant upon the booksellers with whom the orders were placed, or else they sought help from their readers. Accordingly, the collections which were amassed left a good deal to be desired. Other problems encountered were the non-arrival and overdue delivery of books ordered from abroad, and the poor quality bindings of those which did arrive. This meant further delays while the material was sent off for rebinding. Another restrictive factor was the limited range of subject material available.

In order to overcome these problems, staff speaking the relevant Asian languages were sought, for example, the Indian librarian now employed at Wolverhampton both to build up the collections and establish contacts with readers. Rochdale has an official interpreter to help the library in various situations. On the other hand, several communities with a large Asian immigrant population have been unable to appoint suitably qualified staff, and so different methods of solving the problems of book selection and acquisition have been found. At Ealing they have sought the assistance of the Chief Librarian of Delhi Public Library. He has arranged for the purchase of books selected by the Borough Librarian from the list produced regularly for the Library of Congress by the American Libraries Book Procurement Centre in Delhi. The collection at Luton has also been built up with the help of the Delhi Librarian, who has recommended titles and placed orders for those selected. In general, the Library of Congress lists, the Indian National Bibliography (which tends to be a little out of date), and the trade catalogues of Indian and Pakistani publishers are the main selection aids in use. The overall

122

trend is for fewer books to be ordered in this country, and for more reliable contacts to be established with booksellers in the Indian sub-continent. For these reasons sources of supply are improving, and greater use is being made of existing bibliographic tools.

British librarians have been more concerned with the actual provision of books to Asian immigrants than with extension activities. Some librarians of course have made their premises available for cultural events, for instance, at Luton where exhibitions have been held featuring the countries from whence the immigrants have come. At Bradford the public library premises are used for holding talks to Pakistani immigrants on subjects of general interest such as the National Health Service. A good many places organise English language classes but although these are well attended by immigrants, there is a need for better liaison between local librarians and the organisers of the classes. From time to time various promotional measures have been taken in order to draw the attention of immigrants to their local library service. Hence, at Dewsbury the local Pakistani cinema is used to advertise the library's Urdu collection. At Sheffield leaflets were produced in Urdu, and likewise at Rochdale. Booklists and talks have also been used to publicise the library, but in general one senses a certain reluctance to over-publicise the service lest inadequate bookstocks could result in a flood of unsatisfied requests. The real problem is to provide the books, not to promote them.

Extension activities have in the main, been mostly aimed at immigrant children. At Newham a holiday programme was arranged, and at Coventry, thanks to a Home Office grant, a library liaison assistant has been appointed at one of the city's libraries. At Coventry, a reading room has been re-designed for educational and cultural programmes - for films, lectures, music recitals and events related both to life in England and in the immigrant homelands. It has been found, however, that without the presence of a suitably qualified librarian to serve as liaison assistant many such plans can come to naught.

Although they speak, read, understand and write English, Asian children are often still interested in their religious, cultural and literary inheritances from their parents. The result can frequently be a form of 'cultural confusion' between the influence of their more conservative parents, who may have only a slight command of English and whose contact with the host community is slight, and the everyday world of school and work. It is here that librarians must play their part, making the effort to preserve what might be called 'psychological continuity' between the generations. In the event, it will be necessary for immigrant children to have access to good books about their own countries, as well as books in their native tongues. The library should help these children feel a pride in their dual inheritance. In some areas of high immigrant concentration such children can cause problems for librarians. These problems relate not only to the availability of books in appropriate languages (and there is debate still about the desirability of maintaining a 'home' culture by books in the child's parents' language where this language is not English, as opposed to fostering integration by encouraging the use of English language books only), but also to the identification of sufficient and suitable books with a relevant background. The importance of this problem is related not only to the child, but in some cases, to his place as a link with parents who may not feel the need, or desire to participate directly.

As many authorities have large numbers of immigrant children, this has encouraged children's librarians to work more closely, not only with the local education department, but also among themselves. At Bradford, the city library provides a service at eight centres for young immigrants, with elementary readers and a selection of books in English describing the English way of life being made available. In Glasgow, the city's children's librarian is helping a centre for immigrant children which is run by the education department. Groups of children are taken from the centre to the library and enrolled as members, and special collections of books sent out to branches. The books chosen for this purpose have been based on the list drawn up by Birmingham Education Committee (*An exhibition of library books suitable for use with immigrants and linguistically deprived children* City of Birmingham Education Committee, Department for the Teaching of English as a second language, March 1970). In the London area also the problem of providing suitable books for use in schools with a large proportion of immigrant children has been a central one for a small group of children's librarians. The outcome has been the production of an annotated list of books, published in Britain, written for children about the countries from which the majority of immigrant children come. *(Books for Children: the homelands of immigrants in Britain* Institute of Race Relations, 1971.)

So much for the activities of British librarians in general, let us now look at one library in particular where a good deal of work for Asian immigrants is being done, Wolverhampton Public Library. There are over 10,000 Asians within the Wolverhampton area, with a total population of 262,170. The central library has about 2,500 registered Asian borrowers, from a total membership figure of some 20,000 for central. Punjabi is the main language spoken, and there is a large number of Sikhs in the area.

The decision to provide books for these Asian immigrants was taken on his own initiative by the city librarian without the need to consult his committee. To help in serving the Asian population, a graduate Asian librarian was appointed. Although this person helps in the general running of the Central Lending Library his main job is to develop an Asian collection, and so he selects and orders the books, newspapers and records, and answers Asian readers' enquiries at the enquiry desk.

An analysis of the Asian bookstock reveals that as of November 1971, there were 2,175 books in Punjabi, 1,297 in Hindi, and 980 in Urdu. The annual expenditure on Asian books was then about £400, which with the stock as of November 1971 worked out at about 0.33 pence per volume. Total expenditure up to November 1971 was:- on Punjabi books since August 1968 - £711.28; on Hindi books since August 1968 - £463.55; on Urdu books since April 1968 - £328.58. With the exception of a firm in Bradford, all the main book suppliers used by the library are located in either India or Pakistan. The main categories of books ordered; in order of importance of books held by the library are:- novels, poetry and drama; essays; biography; history and geography; philosophy and religion; medicine. In addition to these, dictionaries and encyclopaedias are provided on the shelves of the adult central lending library. The majority of these books are in Punjabi, but each of the categories of book does have three languages represented. The catalogue entries for this material are not very detailed although each of the three languages has its own catalogue drawer. Fiction and non-fiction are intermingled and filed alphabetically by author. These catalogue drawers are placed adjacent to the Asian section in the adult lending library.

The most popular Asian books are fiction and those dealing with religion, while non-Asian works in greatest demand are those dealing with karate, and textbooks in physics, mathematics and chemistry. The library has a good collection of language aids and dictionaries, and there is a section on 'English language for non-English speaking students'. Quite a high proportion of immigrants borrow books in English and the number is steadily growing.

A large number of Asians use the reference library as it is there that the Asian newspapers and magazines are to be found. In fact the reference library has no Asian language books apart from some dictionaries. There are nineteen magazines and newspapers - three in Hindi, five in Punjabi, one in Gujerati, two in Urdu, and eight in English, for instance, *India weekly* and *Pakistan times.* Some of these papers come free in the form of donations, and others are obtained by subscription from a central distribution agency. All in all, there is very little time lag with this material. In addition to these Asian publications, English newspapers are also well used, because the foreign pages in, say *The times* are very good. In general one finds two kinds of Asian users in the Reference Library:- those who want materials in an Asian language, and those who want materials in connection with their studies in English. It is frequently the case that where an Asian comes to the library for information, he will if necessary bring along an English speaking friend to act as translator. This is also the case in the lending departments.

The record library is very well used by Asian members, and there is a constant demand for additions to the stock. The most popular type of music is that from Indian films, and for these records there is always a waiting list. The majority of borrowers are males within the age groups fifteen to forty years. In general it is the teenagers who 'try' the English music, with older members tending to stay with the purely Asian material. The record library also has some music scores and books on music, in relation to the Asian languages. The records are selected through the medium of trade catalogues and, also, as a result of requests from users. The material is ordered through a local department store and takes about three months to come.

Asian children make good use of the library, often bringing with them parents on their first visit to any library. The librarian take the view that all children are the same, regardless of colour

126

or creed, and argues that if this attitude is taken then, in theory, no problems should arise. No special provision for immigrant children is made at the central children's library for it is policy to encourage them to read English. There are some books about India and Pakistan, and efforts are made to acquire works in which the immigrant boy or girl is the main character. The most popular books are folktales, either of their own or other countries, and books about their mother country.

The children's library organises a number of extension activities in which immigrant participation is quite good. There are class sessions in the afternoons for children from local schools (often composed almost entirely of immigrant children), and story hours which are also well supported. However, it is the holiday clubs and the competitions which are really popular with immigrant children and, overall, only a limited number of these children participate in the entire range of extension activities. In fact, it would appear that immigrant children pose no great problems at the central children's library. At the Whitmore Reans branch on the other hand, the membership of the children's section is 50% immigrant and presumably the challenge is somewhat more demanding.

The city librarian takes the view that provision of books and related materials in native languages is likely to go on for at least ten years, but that after that it will taper off. Provision of materials in these native languages is seen as a normal service and not as additional provision. The library has no collections for immigrant use outside its premises, and a collection at one of the local mosques is little used because of its apparent inferiority to the public library stock. A service is given to certain prisons and hospitals, but inmates or librarians have to ask for this, it is not an automatic affair. Wolverhampton does not participate in any scheme of cooperative provision of books in native languages for Asian immigrants, nor does it widely publicise its services.

In overall terms, once the problems of selection and acquisition had been to a large extent diminished through the appointment of an Indian graduate librarian. Wolverhampton Public Library has since faced little or no problems brought about by Asian immigrant use. There have of course been problems general to the city itself, and these have been:- 1 heavy demands made on local authority service, for example, maternity services; 2 the medical

127

problem of tuberculosis, which is common among Asian immigrants; 3 multiple occupation of over 1000 houses in the city; 4 overcrowding of schools in some areas, which leads to a policy of dispersion.

Wolverhampton's education authority works in close cooperation with the public library. There is not only a remedial teaching service, which concentrates on children over the age of thirteen years and those nearing school leaving age, but also a very active language centre. The centre is designed to receive 'new' immigrant children, to teach them to read and to speak English, and then to follow the 'neighbourhood school' policy of putting the children after their course is finished into their local primary or secondary school. The policy is operated because the children concerned know the locality, are situated in an area where the people have the same cultural problems and patterns as themselves, and because it keeps all the children from one family together.

Pupils ages range from eleven to nineteen years and there are basically two kinds of English course at the centre:- 1 a grammatical one, for those going to pursue academic courses such as General Certificate Examinations: 2 conversational English for those going out to work.

All materials used at the centre are graded and structured as children must understand what they are reading or else they lose interest. The reading scheme used is Longmans Structural Readers, although most of the material used in teaching English is produced and printed by the centre itself. This provides for better control and grading of materials. Each class also has its own library which contains books which are all graded. There are also books in the central language laboratory. A certain amount of reading to pupils by staff is carried on as this tends to stimulate interest in reading. Many of the books come from the children's library of the central public library and they are changed quite frequently.

Besides print-based materials the centre uses films, slides and tapes, although again, everything is carefully graded as to ability in English. As well as English the children have classes in such subjects as art, domestic science and gym. English language classes are also held for Asian mothers but attendance at these is both sparse and erratic.

In conclusion, therefore, one would say that all the activities and developments which take place within the library context are very much dependent upon the extent to which librarians are able to make direct contact with the Indian and Pakistani communities. Many towns with large immigrant populations now have voluntary liaison committees which help the librarians in their work. Such committees and their members help bring the library and its services to the attention of local Asian communities. The Community Relations Commission is helping to some extent in bringing this kind of communication about.

The present emphasis is on providing assistance for the immigrants, in order that they may more quickly become adjusted to life in Britain; but communication is a two-way affair. Libraries as one of the media of communication can be used to extend the literary and visual appreciation of the immigrants' cultural background, and to encourage among the host community an attitude that welcomes a pluralistic society in which each of us is willing to 'permit others to be different'.

Many British librarians are concerned about immigrants, and are willing to try to provide them with books and other materials in their native languages, thus making the library a more constructive element in the lives of immigrants. Therefore, while still ill-equipped to tackle the problem in an adequate manner, librarians recognise their responsibility to assist these new ratepayers to become better adjusted to life in their new society. To be effective libraries will have to be innovative and will need to develop special measures to meet these new demands. As a first step the recruitment of staff qualified to cope with at least some of the Indian languages concerned is essential. Moreover, libraries must be willing to allocate a fair proportion of their budgets to tackling this problem. They would do well to remember that there is much more at stake here than the provision of books.

REFERENCES
1 Survey of Asian use of Wolverhampton Public Library carried out by the author in 1971.

LIBRARY SERVICE TO PRISONS IN AUSTRALIA

GORDON KIRBY

Senior Lecturer, Royal Melbourne Institute of Technology

Change in the world of prisons and prisoners is usually slow, and made only in response to pressures which can no longer be ignored. Society for all its pious approval of reform, places a very low priority on the implementation of change. Finance and moral support are reluctantly conceded as they become imperative. In Australia, the tasks of contributing to the pressures for reform, and to the changes themselves, have not been assumed with any great enthusiasm, save by a dedicated few. It is gratifying that among the few are to be found some concerned librarians. What practical help they are able to offer, however, is restricted very much by a lack of understanding of the prevailing situation.

There is very little in print on the subject of prison libraries in this country, although in the six Australian states and the mainland territories (the Australian Capital Territory and the Northern Territory) there are now seventy five prisons. It would, however, be churlish to omit mention of the first article on the subject of prison libraries to appear in the *Australian library journal*. In the ALJ for July 1951, Miss Jean Arnot describes how she and Miss Joan Tighe surveyed the libraries in the prisons of New South Wales, and set up the service very much as it is today.

Of these prisons, New South Wales maintains twenty six; Victoria and Western Australia have thirteen each; Queensland has nine; South Australia eight, Tasmania four, and the Northern Territory two. Prisoners sentenced in Canberra are usually accommodated in prisons in New South Wales, and apart from Aborigines, those prisoners sentenced in the Northern Territory to terms longer than eighteen months, are placed in prisons in South Australia. All prisons are controlled by a state, or territory, government department. In Queensland and Tasmania, it is the Prisons Department; in New South Wales, it is the Department of

Corrective Services; in South Australia it is the recently renamed Department of Corrective Services (formerly the Prisons Department); in Victoria, the Social Welfare Department; and in Western Australia, the Department of Corrections. In the Northern Territory the gaols are administered by the Department of the Northern Territory, an Australian Government agency.

To a certain extent, the changing attitude of the state governments towards prisons and penology is reflected in the nomenclature of the departments, although it would be misleading to conclude that traditional names indicate a hidebound attitude. Most people, including members of the press, have a remarkably archaic view of the Australian prison system. They speak of 'warders', where the modern term is 'prison officers', and 'convicts', where 'prisoners' or 'inmates', is the more acceptable expression; they visualize the inmates as they see them represented in the cinema, on television, or even as depicted in the novels of Charles Dickens. They see 'them' as a race apart, unimaginably violent and depraved, and the 'warders' are viewed as kindly fools at best, or Gestapo-like sadists at worst.

There are several purely sentimental concepts about prisoners, one of which is the, perhaps political, one that all are 'victims' of society, although in what way no one seems to be quite sure. Another view is that of the lonely, frustrated 'birdman of Alcatraz' figure, paying his debt to society over endless years, and working out his own salvation in 'solitary'. In Australia, particularly, the hero worship of Ned Kelly, the man on the run, lends an undeserved glamour to the prisoners that most of us hear about, that is, the escapees. The only thing about these illusions that is basically wrong is that they cloud the real issues, and are of no help to the prisoner in his actual condition. So far as the inmates are concerned, it is probably the case that the majority of prisoners view themselves as people unlucky enough to have been caught doing the same kind of things that most members of 'free' society do also but get away with.

What is seldom realized is that the prison officers are the real captives, tied to jobs with very small salaries, and not too many prospects of career advancement. This is especially true of officers serving in rural areas. No one who has not visited a prison, more especially a maximum security prison, can imagine the tension, the responsibility, and, indeed, the terrors of the prison officer's job.

131

Nor could he understand how little room there is to manoevre in a tight corner between the demands of the regulations, his custodial function, and his own natural reaction to danger. The iniative is almost entirely on the side of the inmate, who has all the advantages, and much of the public sympathy, of the guerilla in any conflict. One has chosen to highlight this, perhaps extreme, aspect of the situation between officers and inmates because it is this ever - present possibility of conflict which creates most of the difficulties for progress and reform, and which especially, places tremendous barriers in the way of librarians attempting to establish a real library service in prisons.

Despite criticism which is often not merely ill-informed, but unjust, there has been a tremendous leap forward in the areas of prison reform, the education of prison officers, and the rehabilitation of prisoners. This has been brought about by the efforts of an enlightened minority which has succeeded in convincing governments and officials that the essential first step in prison reform lies in the education of prison officers for their task. This then has become the top priority. A second step has been the encouragement of prisoners to undertake educational courses, both as a means towards their ultimate rehabilitation and with a view to improving their prospects for employment upon release.

The idea, however, that a library, either within the prison or providing a service from outside, can make a greater contribution to the rehabilitation process is new enough, in Australia, to seem almost revolutionary. The idea, indeed, is not so very well-established, even in countries which lead the world in prison reform.(1) Under these circumstances, the provision of library service assumes a very low priority, particularly in terms of the budget. Libraries, of course, have existed in prisons for decades, although it would be perhaps more accurate to refer to them as collections of books. The very existence of these collections has created certain problems, not the least of which is the assumption that, 'We've got books - of course we've got a library'. Other entrenched ideas are that books are only there for study, or, worse, only for idle moments; or that they exist only to raise the moral tone of the prison. Perhaps this explains why they used to be considered as by nature part of the responsibility of the Education Officer, or even the Padre.

The operation of a library service from outside prison walls presents certain hazards for the librarian, both in respect of providing the books and of recovering them. Several libraries in Australia now provide this service. It is now coming to be recognised that book collections need to be systematized, so that the material may be made available to potential users. In some states, librarians have been appointed with the task of bringing some order to this situation, and of establishing standard library procedures. In others, education officers with a basic grounding in library techniques have been given the additional responsibility of administering the library. In most prisons, however, the task of organising the materials has been given to an inmate, albeit under supervision. The idea that each prison should have a qualified librarian at its disposal is, at present, fantasy of the 'impossible dream' variety.

Prison authorities have limited budgets and large problems; prisoners have to be contained, housed, fed, given work to do, supervised; often they must be escorted (to and from trials, appeals, hospitals or classification, probation or parole interviews), they have to be given medical or psychiatric treatment, counselling, legal aid, and even sometimes special protection. Every item of clothing, of food, and each tool issued, has to be paid for and accounted for. The librarian coming into this situation immediately encounters budgetary problems, security problems, accounting problems, personnel problems and, to a minor extent, censorship problems. Materials for the library quite frequently feature in the budget under headings such as 'incidentals'; book votes tend to vary bewilderingly. One prison officer in conversation with the author, frankly stated that books in a prison were a 'damn nuisance', both because of the question of accounting for them, and of the problems of security. The difficulties of getting a book into a prison where there is tight security would be hard for librarians to conceive, let alone the problems of taking a book out. The loss, theft or destruction of a book can in such circumstances become a truly mountainous molehill. Simply finding somebody, either an officer or an inmate, to administer the issue and return of books can entail a major operation; success is often negated by an unsought transfer or, occasionally, an unexpected departure. It would be wrong, however, to over-emphasize such difficulties, which are in any case, gradually disappearing under more enlightened administrations.

On the question of censorship it is worth stating that there has been in recent years a remarkable relaxation, verging on the permissive. Foreign language materials, once forbidden because the security officer could, perhaps, not assure himself that the material was not obscene or subversive, are now permitted without question. A good deal of soft-core pornography, and even a certain amount of what some would term as hard-core material is permitted. Sensational novels, works on radical politics, indeed, all kinds of material which previously would never have got past the front gate, is now freely admitted; although human nature being what it is, not all of it does get past the gate! Furthermore, works advocating the violent overthrow of authority, or catering to sexual violence and sadism are 'not encouraged' despite such stirring declarations as the following. 'Of course, censorship has no place in prison libraries. Che Guevara and Malcolm X must be allowed to rub shoulders with Winston Churchill, *Portnoy's complaint* with *Tale of two cities*, books on the occult with the books of *The bible*. Prisoners are not children, and neither prison officials nor librarians have a duty to protect them from materials that might confuse or corrupt their tender minds.'(2) The brave statement, however, is made it would seem, without knowledge of the innate conservatism of the great majority of prisoners. In the early 1959s, for example, a prisoner complained that a box of books sent from Pentridge Prison, Victoria, to McCleod Prison Farm in the same state, was full of 'communist literature' and asked for their removal. Indeed, the travelling box library system to the prison was suspended shortly after this incident. The politically radical prisoners are chiefly students and others goaled for evasion of army call-ups, or for activities incidental to protest marches; and it cannot be denied that their ideas have had some small effect upon the reading habits of the other inmates.

Therefore, one of the major problems for the librarian involves a coming to terms with the condition of the job. For the present, at least, it must be accepted that if a service is to be provided, it must be achieved by getting around obstacles rather than by breaking head and heart in trying to remove them. The librarian, then, must become accustomed to the inexplicable rejection of books, budgets, proceedures and sometimes ideas. Compromises are going to be necessary in the realm of acquisition, in technical services and, most particularly, in the area of services to readers.

To most librarians, the idea of library service to prisons probably conjures up a prospect of service to the inmates, and perhaps to their dependants. The government departments which have to meet the cost of any service provided, have a somewhat different approach, which gives priority to the education of prison officers. The needs of the prison staff can be met fairly easily, as the demand is usually for materials wanted in connection with the various training courses available to officers. Where recreational material is required, however, the position is seldom so favourable, and such recreational stocks as exist are provided either by the officer himself or from staff amenities funds. In remote country districts this is no easier for the prison officer than for the prisoner, except during leave periods. Where a prison service is given by the public library, as in Tasmania and the Northern Territory, recreational reading is readily available both to prisoners and staff.

Another problem encountered in the provision of library service to prison officers is that arising from the need to supply certain materials separately from those for inmates. This is required by the prison authorities for reasons of discipline, and also because if an officer and an inmate simultaneously wanted the same volume, the library officer, especially if an inmate, could be put in a distinctly invidious position. This could be a very real possibility in those cases where both inmates and staff are engaged upon similar educational courses, say the Leaving Certificate or the Higher School Certificate. In the more isolated rural prisons, however, this segregation is probably not so rigid, and inmates and staff tend to use the same materials for both study and recration. Moreover, in discussions which the author had with trainee prison officers it was gratifying to see how many of them felt that in any case the prisoner should have prior claim, as the officer could presumably get the material elsewhere.

The second priority in the view of the government departments, is the provision of materials for educational courses taken by the prisoners. This is an area full of pitfalls for the departmental librarian, the first of which is the confusion which exists between textbooks and library materials. It often falls to the librarian to order and supply such textbooks, to house them within the library, and to keep a record of them. Moreover, in Australia, the same textbooks are often not used in consecutive years, and vast amounts of obsolescent materials can be bought, only to be stored or discarded the following year when a new collection is purchased. Textbooks, one would think, should be the responsibility of education officers, who could make use of the librarian's expertise in ordering and arranging the materials. Otherwise, where there is a large number of institutions involved, and a wide choice of course available, this non-library work can consume a disproportionate amount of the librarian's time.

A second pitfall is perhaps illustrated in anecdotal form. A prisoner in an inland institution requested a correspondence course in navigation. The course was approved, the books purchased and sent, and the study begun. The prisoner concerned was transferred to another prison where he commenced a study of boat building. Then, on further transfer to an island prison with a somewhat relaxed attitude towards prisoners' recreation, he put both his courses to good use, and was not recaptured for several weeks after he reached the mainland. This may seem amusing, but the librarian was officially asked to explain how this situation had come about. In general, it may be said that liberal, even lavish, provision is made for prisoners undertaking conventional studies in most prisons. The New South Wales Department of Technical Education, acting in cooperation with the Education Service of the Department of Corrective Services, is developing a range of courses designed to provide vocational skills for inmates; there are ninety five courses listed for men, and twelve for women. Prisoners are encouraged to make use of the Mackay Memorial Technical Library or the Country Reference Section of the Library of New South Wales. There are, however, often irritating and unaccountable delays in obtaining or supplying course material, which on occasion does not arrive until after the prisoner has been released. There is also a fairly high rate of abandonment of courses, owing to loss of interest, transfer to other institutions or discharge. In some cases, inmates who are retarded readers, whether in educational terms or through physical problems such as poor eyesight, undertake courses which they are then unable to complete. Educational officers have often made outstanding contributions towards helping such prisoners, and this is an area where librarians also could develop a special expertise.

Another problem for the librarian is caused by the prisoner who, transferred from one institution to another, wishes to take his library books with him. In some cases, this can be an insuperable problem, even where the request is for the transfer of educational course materials. Nor is this problem noticeably alleviated when the materials concerned are intended for use by the prison staff. What is needed is a general policy for the free movement of books between prisons, which can then be applied consistently. Unfortunately the matter is frequently left to the discretion of individual prison officers or education officers, with results that often appear arbitrary. Apart from anything else the considerable paperwork involved should necessitate the laying down of proper procedures for this operation.

Which brings us to what is probably a third priority of the prison authorities, the provision of recreational reading for inmates. It is now accepted that this material should consist not solely of fiction, and all classes of books are provided. However, it is with this material that the librarian is liable to encounter some of the oddest difficulties. In the first place, there is the general lack of finance for the purchase of new materials. This is not such a problem in New South Wales, where recreational reading for prisoners has been provided on an organized basis for many years. In some states, however, there is as yet no provision for such expenditure; and in others, Western Australia and the Northern Territory for example, the supply is entirely dependent upon outside forces. However, one of the major irritations for the departmental librarian, although not one that is seen as a problem by either the prison authorities or inmate librarians, is the material donated to the prison by well meaning persons and institutions, libraries among them. A great deal of this material is valuable and useful; a very great deal of it is just junk. In the interest of public relations, the departmental librarian must often accept materials which he would not normally consider placing in the library. Often of course, the material arrives at the prison without his knowledge. It may have been solicited by, or accepted by, prison officers or education officers, or requested by inmates who have enjoyed the experience of corresponding with notable persons, and have been rewarded by surprising acts of generosity.(3) A handsome edition of the papers of General Eisenhower graces the shelves of the 'reference' library at Pentridge Prison, Melbourne. On these shelves, however, is where the papers firmly remain.

Some people are quite ruthless in what they dump on unsuspecting, and publicly unprotesting prisoners. Do-good groups promote their causes; book-sellers send obsolete textbooks or remaindered novels which no one ever wanted to read; and unwilling inheritors unload bequests of Victoriana, Edwardiana, and Georgiana, which are of no value, sentimental or otherwise to anybody. At the Fairlea Female Prison, Victoria, someone donated a work entitled, *The use of artificial insemination in pig-breeding;* while a men's prison farm inherited a copy of the *Girls' crystal annual for 1941.* Instances of like absurdities abound, and the librarian should be free to discard such inappropriate material or to find it a better home. On the other hand, some rate, even irreplaceable, Australiana have ended up in Pentridge by way of discard from other libraries. A further almost uncontrollable source of material is that brought in by visitors. In Victoria, for example, visitors may bring to prisoners some half-dozen books or periodicals per month. After this material has been read it tends to circulate among friends and eventually find its way into the library. Being mostly ephemeral material this is rarely recorded or accounted for.

There is the further problem of trying to ascertain the reading requirements of inmates. In some cases, prisoners may ask for reading materials related to their hobbies. On a recent visit to Long Bay Prison, New South Wales, the author noticed that his librarian-escort was thanked for providing some books on tropical fish, and promised two goldfish as a token of appreciation. Knowing one's public is one of the first essentials in providing a good library service, but it is usually extremely difficult to establish any form of direct contact with inmates, although generally they are only too pleased to be of assistance to the visiting librarian. Visits to the institutions are essential if the librarian is to be able to inspect the collections thoroughly, or to deal with such house-keeping routines as evaluating the stock, culling obsolete items, advising on shelving, arrangement and storage, or demonstrating simple loan-and-return procedures to the 'librarian'. In some places, of course, satisfactory means of coping with these problems already exist; but with those institutions at distances of more than one hundred miles from headquarters, such visits can be dauntingly difficult. Even visiting some institutions can bring other difficulties, particularly where the librarian happens to be female. There was a time, indeed, when no female librarian was permitted inside a prison, presumably because of her possible inflammatory impact upon the inmates. There have in fact been some unfortunate cases of attacks made upon visiting entertainers, which may have lent support to this viewpoint. According to hearsay, males have also been 'molested' on visits to female institutions.

It will be seen that the setting up of library systems in prisons can be an enormous task; not least where it involves the harmonising of established systems with current library procedures. Simply managing to take reasonable care of the materials can be challenge enough. It is by no means unique to Australian prisons that books are used for smuggling messages, the keeping of 'accounts' of contraband trading in cigarettes or tobacco, or even, after they have been hollowed out, for the transfer of weapons, money or drugs. Lesser problems arise from the use of endpapers for betting-slips, love-letters, and the like, samples of which have all been discovered in materials withdrawn from prison libraries. Compromise must often be made in the areas of cataloguing and classification. The reduction of subject entries may be seen as a saving of time, cards and drawer space. The classifying of fiction into such groups as thrillers, westerns, sea-stories, romances and the like, must be accepted 'because it's always been done that way'. This can lead to a situation such as obtained at Cooriemungle Prison Farm, Victoria, where everything under thrillers and westerns was read to tatters while books under other classifications grew dusty from nonuse. This situation was to some extent remedied when the fiction was re-shelved alphabetically by author surname.

At first glance, it would seem that the inmate-librarian is the answer to most of the problems encountered in setting up library systems in prisons. On further acquaintance, however, several factors can be seen to militate against success. The first of these is the general lack of library training among prisoners. Conversation with a senior prison officer disclosed that, to his knowledge, no qualified librarian had ever served time in an Australian prison. This lack of training could to an extent be overcome were departmental librarians enabled to train inmates in basic procedures. In New South Wales such opportunities for prisoners to learn the rudiments of library techniques exist in some prisons. In Victoria, it was mooted that a weekend, or even a week, be devoted to such training at Pentridge, with potential inmate-librarians being brought from the country prisons in order to attend. The difficulties involved, notably the problems of obtaining escorts and the lack of instructional materials, eventually led to the abandonment of the idea.

A second factor is the mobility of the prison population. Few prisoners serve their sentences all in one prison, and indeed, it is usually only long term prisoners who are long enough in one place to be of use to a librarian. The great majority of prisoners are short sentence, one time offenders. In metropolitan prisons, a large percentage of the population is composed of unsentenced people; awaiting trial, on remand, awaiting sentence or appeal, or simple unable to raise bail. Only very recently has it been considered that, being technically innocent until proven guilty, such people ought to have accomodation different than that provided for convicted prisoners. These unsentenced people present particular problems in that many of them have nothing to do all day, being perhaps on call for court appearances. There is usually little for them to read apart from periodicals and comics.

A third problem stems from the existence of inmate librarians; although it is perhaps being a little unfair to call this a problem. Many of these people do invaluable work, and if given sufficient guidance and assistance they can perform remarkably well. Many of them become very interested in the work, while inside, although none I have spoken to proposed adopting the profession on release. Which raises a question for librarians; What have you to offer to any ex-prisoner who would wish to work in libraries? It may be of interest to note that in 1970, the Library Association of Australia decided that prisoners of the crown could take the registration examinations, by correspondence, without being members of the association.

In some cases, the job is considered a 'sweet cop', and is jealously treasured by its occupant. In others, as a discharged prisoner once told me, it is considered a job suitable only for, 'schoolteachers and blokes who interfere with kids'. In a manuscript work, anonymous, in the Staff Development Library at Long Bay, New South Wales, appears the observation, 'Homosexual prisoners are too bitchy to be given the three top jobs in the prison, that is, the cook, the librarian, and the medical orderly'.

Some inmate librarians see the departmental librarians as an intruder, and subtly sabotage any efforts to re-systematize the collection. Catalogue cards are 'lost', new books are set aside for favoured friends, art books acquire annotations or are mutilated, and 'pin-up' plates disappear. Much can depend also upon the personalities of inmate librarians, as some examples will illustrate. At Pentridge, in a division for recidivists, the inmate librarian was a silent, sullen man who made toys, and delighted the prison authorities by the immaculate condition in which he kept the stock, which in this section comprised about 1000 books. All had been painstakingly covered in grey or orange cartridge paper, with the short-title neatly printed on the spine; and there they stood in soldierly ranks upon the shelves, arranged by height. This story had a happy ending, however, for the silent one was replaced by a gentle psychotic, who tore off the cartridge paper and restored all the dust-jackets he could find. In some cases, he cut colourful illustrations from womans' papers (by far the most popular material in prisons, as in the home) and used these to enhance the books' appearance. It was odd to see a succulent, impossibly colourful illustration of a 'boeuf Stroganoff' adorning a copy of *The flesh of the orchid,* by James Hadley Chase. Borrowing of the books increased by 400% in eight weeks. In another instance, at McLeod Prison Farm, a 'new broom' inmate librarian who knew his films set aside a shelf of little read materials marked 'Now read the book', with a note of the names of the films made from particular books. Most of these works were borrowed with great enthusiasm.

A great many people are interested in the reading matter of prisoners and this includes prison officers, psychologists, teachers, family and friends. For those without reading problems the answer is simple, they read almost anything which is not physically repellant, that is old, dirty or dull. There are, however, certain steps or stages in their reading interests, of which librarians should take note. For the first-time offender, there is a very considerable 'culture-shock' upon entering prison. There is a great deal òf literature available on the neuroses produced by this experience, which can often be a truly shattering one, but it is not proposed to discuss this here. However, as an inmate librarian of several year's standing told me, the first books a new prisoner wants, as a rule, are law books. Perhaps he feels that his lawyer failed him; perhaps he was undefended; perhaps he wishes to prepare for an appeal against his sentence, or to cope with internal disciplinary 'courts', or to request probation or parole. Alternatively, the problems may concern maintenance, divorce, bankruptcy or company law. Prison authorities offer no objection to stocking this material yet there is the constant complaint that it is never available. One reason for this is its high cost. In Victoria, one work is apparently, essential for court appearances, and this is *Cross on evidence*, which costs around 80 Australian dollars. In New South Wales, there is a small library of legal references available to prisoners, the material having been donated by the New South Wales Penal Reform Council.

The second priority in book needs so far as new prisoners are concerned, is for medical works. Medical care in Australian prisons is of a very high standard, but the new prisoner often develops, or discovers, some symptoms or other. Often he is unwilling to discuss these with either doctors or orderlies, either for personal reasons or because he fears that he may incur some penalty. A supply of popular

141

books in this area would be a boon to many, even at the risk of encouraging malingerers or alarming the suggestable.

A third type of book asked for by prisoners might be what is termed erotica. Again, this covers an area of prisoner-psychology in which one would not presume to claim any expertise. The 'girlie' magazines have their place, no doubt, and some of the more literally descriptive works may serve as vicarious safety valves. In this deeply personal area, one feels that enlightened librarianship would seek a balance, yet would not shirk the task of providing what the inmate requires. The regulations of prison in themselves may tend to counteract such efforts, but often they are not as rigorous as many people believe them to be. Other materials in demand include those covering various hobbies, painting, horse-racing and sport, politics and debating. In womens' prisons, books are supplied on the subject of, for example, home-making, dressmaking, cooking, self improvement, and 'charm'. For the retarded reader which is not to say the retarded intellect, or for the functionally illiterate, or the intellectually handicapped, library provision becomes very much a question of cooperation between librarian and education officer. Prison is not infrequently, the first place where men find time, and sufficient interest, to read seriously. An acquaintance tells of his stay in hospital, where his neighbour cheered his convalescence by extensive recitals of Shakespeare, spoken with deep feeling and understanding. One day he revealed that he had acquired this love for, and knowledge of, the great Elizabethan's work while in prison.

The greatest problem for the departmental librarian lies in the question of reference service, both for prisoners and staff. At present, efforts are made to answer questions, usually directed through the education officer, and to prepare brief bibliographies or reading lists. Often moreover, the loan of these recommended materials can be arranged. Even here one must be careful however. An English librarian, now in South Australia, told of supplying Burke's *Peerage* and other biographical works for a prisoner in England. He was gently discouraged on learning that the prisoner concerned was a notorious confidence-man preparing for his imminent return to the outside world.

Some attempt is also made at the provision of current awareness services, but the 'harvest indeed is great', and such enterprise usually founders on the rock of staff-shortages. This is, potentially, the area where the public libraries could offer most help, and indeed, in Tasmania and Western Australia, both of which have centralized

142

state-wide library services, either public libraries or the State Library provides such a service. In other states, librarians have reiterated their willingness to do likewise.

At a more general level, the task of providing a library service in the prisons of Australia continues, with a good deal of variation as between the individual states. Indeed, such is the extent of this variation that it is worth giving a brief summary of the current position in each of the states. In New South Wales, a start has been made by creating the position of librarian to the Department of Correctional Services. Seconded from the Library of New South Wales, this person is located at the Long Bay prison complex, where there are four prisons. She administers the Staff Development Library, the Mackay Memorial Technical Library and the Accessions Centre. The Staff Development Library, established in 1971, contains about 3,500 books, mainly in the fields of social welfare and criminology, and it is used mainly by education officers, prison officers, probation and parole officers, and psychologists. A letter from Miss Lorraine Purcell, the librarian, discloses that the collection covers psychology, behaviour, sociology, social welfare, criminology, corrections and management. Loans average about ninety a week, and a photocopying service is available for journals, which are not lent. The librarian has compiled a printed catalogue, which has been mimeographed and made available to other institutions. The Mackay Memorial Technical Library now contains over 50,000 books, in the main, multiple copies of texts used in connection with the educational courses available to the prisoners. Most of these books are issued on extended loan for the duration of the course concerned, and they range from elementary textbooks in reading and writing to university-level material. An average of one hundred books is sent out by rail every week.

The Accessions Centre at Long Bay is a replacement for a similar facility destroyed during a riot at Bathurst Gaol during February 1974. In this riot, the entire library stock of 2,500 books was destroyed, along with 48,000 record cards indicating the whereabouts of other books within the prison system.(4) These records are slowly being re-compiled by photocopying the cards held at each institution. As replacements, some 10,000 volumes have been purchased, mostly in multiples of ten, in order to reduce the cataloguing problems and to speed up delivery of stock to the twenty six prisons in the system.

In 1972, there were twenty five prisons for men in New South Wales, and two institutions for women, one a pre-release centre housing only ten women. This overall figure includes five training centres and six afforestation camps. In 1972, the daily average prison population was 4,163 persons; the daily average of unsentenced persons was 518.5. However, receptions from the courts totalled 20,790, a figure which included persons received more than once. There is quite a range of industrial activity within this prison system including matmaking, bookbinding, brushmaking, garment work, and rural primary production. The range of educational courses available is even wider, embracing all levels of course from elementary to university standard, and providing ample choice to both men and women prisoners. The range includes: basic education, secondary education, university courses (arts at Macquarie and New England Universities), electrical trade, building trade, printing, commerce and management, plus such rural activities as bee-keeping, dairy technology, and wool classing. For women, classes cover, drama, art, embroidery, cake decorating, first aid, gardening, hairdressing, millinery, pottery, typing and weaving.

In the larger prisons, libraries are usually run by a prison officer with the assistance of some of the prisoners. In smaller institutions they are often run by prisoners alone. The total bookstock within the New South Wales prison library system is estimated at around 55,000. Book selection is the responsibility of the departmental librarian. A wide variety of interests and levels is catered for, although material dealing with arms and explosives is not encouraged. Books on handicrafts are always popular, and prisoners may usually borrow three volumes a week. Periodicals and popular magazines are received on subscription at most prisons, and the lists include old standards such as *National geographic* and the *Readers' digest*. The librarian has recently submitted a request for a bookmobile in order to transfer materials between institutions.

Queensland has as yet no departmental librarian at the Prisons Department. The state's nine prisons include two at Rockhampton, one of which sometimes houses female prisoners, as does the female division of Brisbane Prison. Queensland has accomodation for 1,094 male and 722 female prisoners, a total of 1,816. During the year 1974, some 5,035 prisoners were received by the system, and 5,208 discharged, leaving 1,401 still in confinement. More than half of these prisoners are held at Brisbane, where the daily average prison population is 651, half of whom are women. The other prisons at Rockhampton, Townsville, Wacol, Woodford, for young offenders, Numinbah and Palen Creek concentrate in the main upon agricultural activities. Wacol also has a Security Patients' Hospital, where psychiatric and medical services are provided. At Brisbane, an average of forty prisoners attended primary classes during 1973, with a further forty five engaged upon secondary studies, and four enrolled for university or certificate studies. Other courses offered include, music, home gardening and animal husbandry. A remedial teacher provides tuition for illiterate and slow learning prisoners.

Libraries exist at each of the prisons, although the one at Woodford is of very recent vintage. Townsville and Rockhampton public libraries provide bulk lending services to their respective prisons, and at the former, some 200 books are lent and issued monthly. Requests for particular items are answered. No periodicals are lent, and no discard materials donated, for as one librarian observed, 'I wouldn't want to, it's like giving second-class material to second-class people'.(5) The Extension and Circulation Service of the State Library of Queensland provides a service to the state's prisons. Within the prison library service itself, funds for each institution are provided on an annual basis. The total bookstock in 1973 was estimated at 12,000 and, every type of normal acceptable literature is available to inmates.(6) Each institution is served by an inmate librarian.

In South Australia too there is no librarian on secondment to the Department of Correctional Services, although there is a library at the department's office in Adelaide. The State Library of South Australia provides advice and cooperation at all levels however. Of the eight prisons in the state, five are at country centres. The daily average of prisoners in 1973 was 931, made up of 891 men and 40 women. The average monthly enrolment for prisoners on courses was 196.2; for primary courses 15, for technical courses 77.3, for secondary courses 46.2. Private study occupied an average of 36.7 persons. A survey in 1972, found that of 339 members of staff in the South Australian Prison system, about twenty officers at all levels were pursuing studies, both of an external nature and within the aegis of the staff-training scheme.

In South Australia, education officers play a large part in the purchase and distribution of library books for both inmates and staff. There are libraries at every prison, and in June 1973, the total bookstock was estimated at 15,600. At this period there were 835 prisoners.(7) In addition to such recreational activity as reading there is a range of industrial activity which includes baking, laundry work, sheetmetal work and a variety of agricultural pursuits. The largest collection of books is at Yatala Labour Prison, where there are 6,000 volumes. Next comes the gaol at Adelaide with 3,500 books. Seventy five percent of all these books are purchased items. Although there are no law books in any of the libraries, these may be borrowed from the State Law Society.

The State Library of South Australia also helps with a lending service to prisons. For several years this was provided only to Yatala, but now more institutions have been persuaded to avail themselves of the Adult Lending Service of the State Library. Bulk loans of 400 books are sent regularly to Yatala; loans of 100 or more to smaller institutions. These books are changed regularly every five or six months, although institutions may if they so desire, have as few as twenty replaced at any one time. Withdrawn books are not donated to Correctional Services establishments.

In Tasmania also, there is no secondment of a librarian from the State Library to the Prisons Department, although libraries in the island's four prisons are supervised by the State Library's External Services Librarian. Of the four prisons, two are at Risdon, near Hobart, one at Launceston, and the other, the Kilderry Farm Gaol, is at Hayes. In 1973, there were 380 prisoners, ten of them in the female division at Risdon. Accomodation exists for 440. Educational courses are offered, and these are administered entirely by the educational department. The education officer arranges for the supply of all necessary textbooks. In-service training is offered to the staff but, in general, it has not been found necessary to provide a library service for them.

Libraries exist in all the prisons except Launceston. Recreational reading material is provided entirely by the External Services Department of the State Library, save for a small percentage of donations, which is less than ten percent of the total bookstock. There are about 8,000 books within the system, 6,000 of which are in the male division at Risdon. The State Library provides assistance with cataloguing and answers reference enquiries. Internal borrowing is recorded by inmate librarians, while the education officer acts as liason with the State Library.

In the State of Victoria there is a departmental librarian, in this case at the time of writing the post is empty. The job of the departmental librarian is based upon the library of the Social Welfare Training Institute. Victoria has thirteen prisons, seven of which are training institutions, including the Fairlea Female Prison. During 1972-73, these prisons accomodated a daily average of 2,096 prisoners, 33 of whom were women. Accomodation exists for 2,414 men and 100 women, but with only 19 women prisoners in 1974, Victoria is considering abandoning imprisonment for women offenders. There are two open prison farms, two afforestation camps, one semi-hospital prison, and one rehabilitation centre, Over half the state's prison population is held at Pentridge.

The training prisons provide courses for inmates, and in 1972-73 there were sixteen education officers, all teachers from the State Education Department. There were also nine trade instructors in prisons. Bookstock in these prisons consists partly of material supplied by the Social Welfare Department and partly of stock from the public libraries. Between 1962 and 1968, more than 3,500 books, all fully catalogued, were supplied by the former complete with cards. Funds then dwindled and no recreational material at all has been purchased recently. A great deal of donated material reaches each prison, not all of it readable. Public library support has also been evident. Sale and Morwell River prisons have both had large donations from this source, while the Bendigo City Librarian helps to catalogue materials in the Bendigo Training Prison library. The Coburg City Library, situated within a stone's throw of Pentridge, offers a reference and loan service through the education officer. The State Library gave generously of discarded books in the past, and it still provides a reference service upon request.

At Pentridge Prison, soon to be divided into three separate institutions, there are ten separate libraries. Two of these are in 'A' division, where the general library contains about 10,000 books, and the La Trobe Reference Library, founded to aid the highly-successful La Trobe Debating Club, has about 2,000. Other divisions have about 500 to 1,000 books each, many of which are paperbacks or books donated in the Pentridge prison library system. Pentridge also has its own collection of gramophone records, donated by radio stations, which are used on the prison's internal broadcasting system. Some serials are supplied to each prison for recreational purposes.

In Western Australia there has been a request to have a librarian seconded to the Department of Corrections, although such an appointment has not yet been made. Of the state's eleven prisons, the largest one is at Freemantle. In 1970-71, it had an average prison population of 499.2. In the state as a whole there were, in June 1971, 1360 prisoners, of whom 406 were aboriginal men, and 52 aboriginal women, 668 white Australian men and 19 women. The remainder being 'other nations' whites and 'other nation's coloured'. Most aborigines were imprisoned for drunkenness and stealing, while most of the non-aboriginals were locked up for stealing and drunkenness.(8) About 200 prisoners were taking courses in 1974, most of them by correspondence, but some through attendance at technical schools. Art teachers and trade instructors give instruction in prison, and there are also courses for illiterates. Legal materials can be obtained as requested.

There is a Central Research Library of about 660 books and thirty serials, covering criminology and sociology. It is used by prison staff and by some people from outside, such as tertiary students, probation and parole officers. The library is at present run by three postgraduate psychology students. There is also a Staff Training Library of about 400 books. In the prison system as a whole, there is an estimated bookstock of 15,600; of these about seventy five percent are purchased and perhaps five percent sent privately to prisoners. Of the libraries, nine are run by a single inmate, one has two inmates in charge, and another is run by a nurse assisted by two inmates. The Freemantle Public Library has donated discard materials, and has helped to classify the book collection at the Freemantle Prison. An informal reference service is provided via prison or education officers. Banbury Rehabilitation Centre belongs to the State Circulating Library and is able to change 120 books every month. In Kalgoorlie, the famous inland mining town, inmates can go to the town library to borrow books.

The two gaols in the Northern Territory are supplied by the Darwin Public Library, which is substantially assisted by the National Library of Australia. These prisons are at Farnie Bay, Darwin, rumoured to have been host at one time to the late Errol Flynn, and recently destroyed by a tornado, and at Alice Springs. No information has been available about educational courses for either prisoners or prison officers. Loans to both the Alice Springs and Darwin Gaols increased substantially during the late 1960's and early 1970's so far as one can ascertain, although again documentation is scanty.

As is customary after a survey such as this, one is tempted to draw some conclusions as to what can be done to improve the general level of the prison library service. Although the provision of more money by the governments concerned would be the first suggestion that would come to mind, there are certain more practical measures which can be taken by librarians wishing to make a contribution in this area:-
1   Where there is no departmental librarian, to work for the

appointment of a qualified person to such a position. 2 To work in collaboration with the departmental librarian to obviate duplication of effort. 3 To send all donation materials to a qualified librarian, in order thay they may be used to the greatest advantage. 4 To exercise some discernment in the choice of such materials. 5 To offer some practical assistance with library procedures in the prison itself; this means, in fact, arranging to spend some of one's own leisure time doing this type of work. 6 To establish good relations with the local prison authorities, especially the education officers. 7 To establish, in collaboration with the departmental librarian and the prison authorities, set procedures whereby prisoners may as individuals make use of the lending and reference service offered by the library. 8 To consider the question of the employment of prisoners in the library on 'work release'; and to consider the question of employment for the discharged prisoner.

REFERENCE

1   There are numerous articles expressing this point of view in American journals, particularly in *American libraries* and the *Wilson library bulletin.*

2   Des Pickering and Helen Modra *Library services to the disadvantaged: a report to the nation* Melbourne, Australian Library Promotion Council 1973, 29.

3   See articles by a Kevin in *Stockade* 7, 4, June 1963 and *Stockade* 8, 2, March-April 1964.

4   *Daily telegraph* Sydney February 5 1974.

5   From a conversation with Mrs J G Brent, Librarian of Townsville Municipal Library.

6   Response to a questionnaire sent by Helen Modra, June 29 1973.

7   Response to a questionnaire sent by Helen Modra, June 18 1973.

8   The exact figures are:

	Stealing	Drunkenness
Whites	1233	1166
Aboriginals	323	1406

TWO PRISON LIBRARIES IN SWEDEN

LENNART ENGE

Librarian in charge of the prison libraries at
Hall and Haga, Sodertatje, Sweden

Since the correctional system provides the background for the library service Hall and Haga, it is perhaps advisable to begin with a brief description of the Swedish correctional system. There are approximately 70 prisons in Sweden, with a total of about 5,000 places, although the number of people in prison at any one time is generally around 4,000. In comparison with English and American prisons those in Sweden are very small, the biggest having 450 places. These institutions are divided into various categories according to the type of punishment being applied. The principal forms of punishment are imprisonment, juvenile imprisonment, and internment, with the latter differing from imprisonment in that it is a more serious sentence, open-ended in nature, and imposed only for repeated criminal activity. Until very recently the prisoners have been kept apart with, for example, only internees going to an internment institution, and so on. However, recent prison reforms have meant that prisoners will no more be segregated according to sentence. From now on there will be two kinds of prison, local prisons for juvenile and short-term offenders, and national prisons for long-term offenders and internees. The state is entirely responsible for the Swedish penal system which it operates through the National Correctional Administration.

Prison society differs in many respects from the greater society outside prison walls, and these differences affect the provision of library services as they do all aspects of prison life. It is hoped that the following description of the two institutions where the author works, Hall and Haga, may provide an illustration of conditions in prison, and the manner in which these influence the work of the library.

These two institutions are located to the south of Stockholm and lie about two kilometres apart. Hall is an internment institution with room for 350 people, and most of the complex is surrounded by walls. In the centre of this complex, inside the walls, is a large factory building itself encircled by residential blocks. These residential blocks are themselves separated from each other by a series of walls. In addition to these buildings there is a special medical unit, for psychiatric as well as ordinary medical care, a reception unit, and an isolation unit. Used in this context isolation means solitary confinement. These separate sections of the institution are connected by a subway. Outside the walls are the so-called open sections, where the prisoners have outside employment, and life is subject to fewer regulations.

Haga is a small prison which holds fifty inmates and serves as a psychiatric hospital for the whole Swedish correctional system, although there are also small psychiatric units in certain other prisons, for instance, at Hall. Besides the external precautions which are designed to prevent anyone from escaping, there are also internal restrictions on the lives of the prisoners. One of these is compulsory work from which only the sick and those attending the prison school are exempt. Periods of communal leisure are brief and, apart from mealtimes and the daily exercise session between 12.00 and 1.00 pm when prisoners are taken out into the yard, all communal activity ceases with the end of the daily leisure period which lasts from 5.00 pm until 7.00 pm. Shortly before 8.00 pm, the prisoners are locked in their cells for the night.

In recent years there have been signs of a certain easing of conditions in prison, and whereas previously, prisoners were rather cut-off from the outside world, the picture is no longer so bleak. Thus, excursion and discussion groups are now appearing in most prisons, while another feature is visits by drama companies with, afterwards, a general discussion of the performance in which the prisoners can join. As for the excursion groups, these are comprised of ordinary citizens who visit prisons on a voluntary basis, sometimes showing films, and sometimes organising discussion groups. They help the prisoners to keep in touch with the outside world. At Hall, one notable improvement has been the prison school which, although situated within the walls, is staffed by teachers from outside who are not prison employees. Last, but by no means least, there is the added attraction of the library, which unfortunately, remains a somewhat singular blessing, as

151

library service of the Hall and Haga type is not common in Sweden. At the time of writing, the Hall and Haga librarian is the only librarian working on a fulltime basis in any prison. It had originally been the intention to extend the Hall and Haga type of library service to all prisons but, owing to a lack of finance, very little has been done in this direction.

All this represents a considerable penetration of prison life by the outside world. These improvements should not be regarded as isolated phenomena but must be seen in the light of a newly-awakened consciousness and will to resist on the part of the prisoners. Prisoners began to organise themselves towards the end of the 1960s in order to create the basis for a critique of the correctional system. This critique even took the form of protest action, of strikes of various kinds. Being conscious through their own experience of the negative effect of imprisonment, the prisoners sought by their demonstrations to bring about such long-term improvements as more lenient conditions of parole, the abolition of compulsory work, and better opportunities for visiting. Their long-term aim is the abolition of prisons. At the present time, the prisoners have been forced on to the defensive because, in the wake of the drug problem, politicians and public opinion in general have adopted more repressive attitudes.

Such was the background to the library service which was introduced at Hall and Haga on an experimental basis in 1968, and which is now a permanent feature at both institutions. The original three-year project was designed to provide some indication of the demand for a prison library service and also to test several aspects of the service, such as a lending service, and various cultural services. It was intended that the results of the study be used later as a basis for the expansion of the entire Swedish prison library system. The project was influenced by the efforts of the prisoners,and particularly by their demand that they should receive the same standard of library provision as was available to all other citizens. For this to be so, it was emphasised that the prisoners should have free and direct access to the books, that is that there should be no censorship.

The project was organised on a cooperative basis, with the town of Sodertalje providing the service through its local library, and the costs being borne by the National Correctional Administration. Operations began with the introduction of a book bus driven by a librarian, which made the rounds of the various prison blocks to a timetable which gave every prisoner the opportunity of visiting the library at least once a week. Gradually, in addition to the usual library services, other facilities were introduced. These included film shows, visits from writers, musical evenings, plays, exhibitions and, before the general election of 1970, a political discussion in which representatives of the political parties took part. At the end of the experimental period, in August 1971, a survey of library use was carried out amongst the prisoners in Hall. Approximately seventy five percent of the prisoners claimed to make regular use of the service. In answer to questions about the kinds of books that they preferred to borrow, it emerged, not surprisingly, that adventure stories, war novels, and travel books came top of their list, with science fiction, medicine and religion coming at the other end of the scale. All in all it can be said that during this experimental phase, the library service became firmly established in both institutions, and that the subsequent development of the service along somewhat different lines, was to a large extent based upon the experience of this trial period.

One of the most important features of this revised library system is the library bus, which still comprises the basis of the book lending service. This arrangement is somewhat artificial in that a bus is by no means the most natural environment for the provision of a library service. Nevertheless, there are advantages as well as disadvantages, and it is a point in favour of the bus that it provides a means of reaching all the prisoners with the exception of those in special categories, who are visited by car. This arrangement would be impossible given a fixed location library because, in the first place, one is dealing with two separate institutions a considerable distance apart and, secondly, because the security risk created by the presence of large numbers of prisoners would prohibit free access to the library. Prisoners from different categories have not until the recent prison reform been allowed to meet during their leisure period. Under previous circumstances, at least three library buildings would have been required if the bus was to have been completely replaced. For the future, a mixed system would be preferable, so that most of the prisoners in Hall would have a fully-equipped library building, while at the same time, Haga and the remainder of the prisoners in Hall, who comprise: those living in the open units, who are not

153

allowed to go inside the walls; those living in the isolation units, who are not allowed to enter the library because of their isolation; and those who are in the medical unit, would obtain their library service through the medium of the library bus. Admittedly such a system would still not remove the disadvantages of the library bus, principal among which is the limited scope of the service it can provide, which again stems from the isolation of prison life and the fact that the bus has no newspapers, reference works or facilities for listening to records.

Under the present system, once a week in the hour-long exercise period, the library bus is parked at the door of the appropriate section, that is, there is a different day for visiting the different categories of prisoner. The prisoners then come to the bus, without any special security measures, and they can choose freely from the book shelves. The bus only carries about 1,000 books, half of which may be classified as light reading, the other half as non-fiction. Naturally, such a limited stock of books cannot hope to meet the demands put upon it, and the author keeps a check on requests which the bus stock cannot satisfy and attempts to obtain these from the town library. Many of these volumes are, however, not to be found in the town library, for example, books in Arabic, older Swedish literature, or advanced subject literature, and for such subjects the interlending machinery is used. At times readers ask for follow-up material to works requested earlier, and this can put the expertise of the librarian greatly to the test. On occasion also, assistance in these matters is forthcoming from the other prisoners, some of whom appear to be bafflingly well-informed. In order to keep the readers as well-informed as possible, lists of recent library acquisitions are distributed among them. In addition, many of the prisoners use specialised subject biblio-graphies, as well as the book review sections of newspapers. As there is neither an alphabetical or a classified subject catalogue in the book bus, the author himself occasionally compiles lists of titles covering a special theme, for example, biographies of a particular writer, the protection of the environment, or the uses of nuclear energy. The issue system in operation is the same photographic process as is used in the town library, with each reader having a ticket just as in the town service. If this sounds like a somewhat bureaucratic procedure there are, nevertheless, good reasons for it. In the first place, it is a very useful means of supplying sceptical outsiders with accurate statistics on the number of books borrowed; secondly, it is easier to trace reserved books where such a system of control exists.

The reading interests of people in prison are no less varied than are those of ordinary library users. As has already been indicated, roughly half of the books on loan would be described as 'light reading' and the rest as non-fiction. Typical examples of the leisure reading of prisoners are the works of Desmond Bagley, Alistair Maclean and Jack London, and books about war. Modern English novels are the most popular books in the library and, indeed, some sixtyfive percent of all fiction issues are works by foreign authors. There is a definite tendency to avoid reading the work of Swedish authors, and the explanation for this is probably to be found in a desire on the part of the prisoners to escape from the miserable reality of their own lives. Hence they tend to avoid Swedish milieux and society. The demand for works of non-fiction is extremely varied, with sport, technology, politics, travel, natural sciences and art all being very popular. In the case of art books the most popular volumes are large folios with colour reproductions, which probably reflects a need for colour in the drab surroundings of prison. Moreover, many of the prisoners are themselves painters, and for this reason make heavy use of the art books. All in all then, the reading situation in Hall and Haga is greatly similar to that which obtains in the outside world. The basic difference lies in the quantity of books available on loan.

The prisoners in fact read a great deal, and one would like to demonstrate this with reference to the lending statistics of the last five years. the situation is as follows:-

Year	Number of volumes issued
1969	23,807
1970	29,386
1971	29,867
1972	38,221
1973	37,047

During 1973 there were on average some 321 prisoners in both institutions, which means that for that year alone, an average of 115 books per head were issued. The prison staff on occasion voice the fear that a great many books will go missing or even be stolen. This is not the case, for the proportion of missing books has always been less than one percent of the total number out on loan. Anyway, if the demand for a service is present, such arguments even where they carry more validity than this one, ought not to be the predominant consideration. The foregoing statistics, figures for the past five years, show that the interest in reading at Hall and Haga is no chance phenomenon, no mere passing phase.

The system of book supply at both Hall and Haga is a perfectly normal one and there are no special conditions or proscriptions. Indeed, as the material emanates from the town library, book selection for the two institutions is subject to exactly the same criteria as is that for the town. There is no censorship as the prison authorities at national level decided some years ago that all printed materials available for sale should be accessible to the inmates of the prisons. Furthermore, in order to satisfy the demand for any material which might be of particular interest to the prisoners, duplicate copies of all books in this category are purchased. Examples which come to mind are career literature, books about social welfare services, dictionaries and novels such as *Papillon* by Henri Charrier. Moreover, so far as is practically possible, other materials such as periodicals, newspapers and language courses on tape and record are put at the disposal of the prisoners. In Hall, the biggest obstacle so far as audio-visual teaching aids is concerned, lies in the fact that prisoners are not allowed to have tape recorders or record players in their cells. As usual, the reason given for such restrictions is the familiar one of order and security. Specifically, the authorities have feared that tape recorders and record players would afford obvious hiding places for both narcotics and weapons. At Hall, there is a record player in the school which means that at least the pupils have an opportunity to listen to records from the library. Happily this situation does not arise at Haga, where the prisoners borrow from 300 to 400 records every year.

The record player is not the only point of contact between the prison school and the library service. Although the school pursues certain formal educational goals, which the library does not, in both practical and ideological terms we are in agreement. For various reasons, most of the prisoners have great gaps in their education, and an attempt to fill these is made in the form of two courses, the lower of which corresponds in level to that of classes one to three in the normal school. (By normal school is meant the Swedish comprehensive school, which has nine classes. The level here referred to is that of the three highest classes in the school.) At any one time an average of about thirty pupils to be found attending the school. A great deal of emphasis is put on group activity, especially in the higher course, which while not directly vocational, attempts in a general way to prepare the inmates for later vocational training when they leave prison. A practical demonstration of the cooperation which exists between library and school can be given with reference to a group activity entitled 'The three villages'. In this, life in three villages is described, and these are a Swedish village, a Tunisian village, and a Chinese village. The reading material for this project all comes from the local public library, and when the work is completed an exhibition on the theme is mounted in the town library. Each semester, the author takes two-hour long study sessions in which the primary aim is to draw attention to those modern library facilities which it is not possible for the library bus to provide, such as newspapers, periodicals, records, a general information service and so on. Above all, the aim is to prevent any vestige of the state institutional image from being attached to the library service, for it must be remembered that the prisoners have unpleasant memories of other public institutions such as police stations and law courts. At the prison school there is also a little bookstand holding about 200 volumes, which is maintained by the Sodertalje Public Library. The contents of this stand are regularly attuned to the content of the school curriculum.

Although the provision of a lending service and an information service represent the basic functions of a library, the concept of library service has broadened a great deal over the years to include such activities as exhibitions, performances and other cultural events. Literary material can be brought to life through the media of films, dramatic performances, lectures, exhibitions, and visits by authors. By such means the librarian can highlight current social problems or communicate artistic experience. These aspects of library service are particularly important in prison, as they offer the prisoners a link with the outside world. Cultural activities were introduced into both Hall and Haga during the experimental stage. There was no thought of entering into competition with the existing leisure schedules of the two institutions, but rather the intention was to supplement these activities and to offer an alternative to them.

The present prison leisure programme is in fact somewhat limited in that, the films especially, tend to be of the blood and thunder variety. Since the onset of the library service, fifty films have been shown under the auspices of the library. The emphasis throughout has been on the choice of good films irrespective of their content. Most of the films shown have been Swedish ones, but the inclusion of such foreign productions as *Fahrenheit 451, Catch 22, Playtime* and *Dr Strangelove* may be cited as evidence of the wide ranging nature of the library film programme. As for the prisoners, not only have they accepted this rather more difficult repertoire but, indeed, they have asked for the library film shows to be continued. Moreover, as film shows can very easily degenerate into passive imbibing of whatever happens to be on the screen, expert film critics are always on hand to discuss the contents of the film with the prisoners. These are people who write film reviews for the local newspaper, and their function in this case is to initiate a general discussion about the film at the end of each performance. These discussions are usually wide ranging, which is a good thing because it is often in this way that someone discovers that 'this is really relevant to me', or learns that other people hold views similar to his own. Such discussions are not confined to the contents of film shows, and often occur after plays, to which indeed, they are a natural follow-up, since with the actors actually present it is possible to have a direct exchange of views between audience and cast.

One would emphasize the need for this kind of prisoner participation because so often productions of this type may be used as agents of pacification, serving only to reinforce the oppressive atmosphere of prison. Consequently, every effort must be made to counteract the effects of the daily prison routine of eating, working and sleeping, without at the same time succumbing to the illusion that by such means one is able to remove the actual condition of imprisonment. Therefore, prisoners are constantly encouraged to make use of the library, and to attend cultural events, in the belief that such activities lead to increased self-awareness and to a broader outlook on life. In this connection the author must mention a project begun by his predecessor. He wrote to practically every organisation which produced posters, for instance, theatres, museums and art galleries, asking for samples to hang on the walls of the long subway in Hall. As a result the subway, with its colourful posters, was transformed into an underground gallery. Now the corridors in Haga are similarly decorated. Posters which are not used are distributed among the prisoners so that they may have a little colour inside as well as outside their cells.

The effects of such activities may be seen, for example, in the book and theatre reviews which appear in the Hall prison newspaper. Haga, unfortunately, lacks such a publication. However, this is only one side of the coin, and the other is that contact with people from the outside results in a two-way process of communication. It is significant that through meeting the prisoners, sensitive people such as for example, writers, become to a certain extent eye-witnesses of imprisonment. Thus it came about that a drama group which had visited Hall on several occasions, was moved to write a play about prisons, which it subsequently performed in schools. Unfortunately, such a positive exchange of ideas and understanding is never easy to achieve, basically because of the restrictions imposed by the need for order and security. It is the dictates of security that keeps prisoners apart during the leisure period, or rather has done until recently. In Hall this also led to a system of double showings of films, since all prisoners were not allowed to attend at the same times.

Prisoners are a disadvantaged group in society, but the rules which apply to other disadvantaged groups, whose right to the help and support of society is recognised at least in principle, do not seem to apply to them. Prisons are still inhumane institutions whose main purpose is to lock people away, people for whom the path back to society is not made easy. The high rate of recidivism proves this. To combat this development, prisoners should have the opportunity to make up what they missed at school, to be trained for a job suited to their individual capacities, rather than to have to waste their time sewing mailbags, and to make contact with people outside the walls. Included in this general statement of aims is the right to an efficient library service as a source of knowledge, information and entertainment. Furthermore, bigger libraries than at present exist are required, libraries which are just as well-equipped as any public library, with books, newspapers, periodicals, tapes, discs, slides and whatever else may be needed. Included in this would be qualified library staff, people with the ability to provide a professional information and readers' advisory service, in addition to dealing with the lending and recreational demands of the readers. Naturally, such staff must also be very well acquainted with the prison system. Finally, the tremendous interest shown by prisoners in exhibitions, film shows, dramatic performances, and visits by writers, highlights the need to provide more discussion during the leisure period. In short, a multi-purpose library service is required such as would offer the prisoners the opportunity of escaping from passive resignation, and of broadening their horizons. It could also, hopefully, give them a greater incentive to put their criminal ways behind them, and strengthen their resolve, once their debt to society has been paid, never to return to prison.

LIBRARY SERVICES TO IMMIGRANTS IN AUSTRALIA

T THOMAS

Formerly Law Librarian, University of Sydney
now consultant to Macquarie University Library.

Australia has been a country of immigrants since its inception in 1788, the original inhabitants, other than the aboriginal people, being convicts, military men, and some free settlers and administrators. These people were almost entirely of British stock. Non-British immigration did not begin in earnest until the years preceeding the second world war and received its greatest impetus under the Chifley Labour Government immediately after the war. The policies then laid down were continued under subsequent non-Labour administrations up to the end of 1972. Immigrants at first were mainly English-speaking and white, with a strong bias towards men and women from the United Kingdom and other parts of the British Commonwealth. 'Foreigners' did come but in lesser numbers and again they were white and of European stock. The need to fill Australia's so called empty spaces, to undertake the rapid expansion of manufacturing industry, and to compensate for a not very vigourous birth rate, were amongst the factors which motivated the stepping-up of immigration. In addition, there were numbers of people, particularly in Europe, who wanted to make a fresh start in the 'Land of Opportunity'. Still the greatest numbers were from the United Kingdom, some sponsored, some specially recruited and encouraged by generous government assistance with passages. Yet these were not enough, so recruitment was expanded to include non English-speaking peoples on the European mainland. This enabled Australia to fill its migration targets and, at the same time, pursue humanitarian goals amongst the thousands of displaced people and refugees fleeing from regimes politically obnoxious to them.

The result of the various immigration programmes is that in 1975, one person in every five in Australia was born outside the country. Of these 'New Australians' as they are sometimes called,

161

the greatest number is English-speaking. Since 1972, there has been a slight watering down of the old 'White Australia' policy, and persons from the Pacific area, Africa and Asia have been admitted with strict controls over numbers and suitability. The present Labour administration has, for a variety of reasons, some economic, some ideological, some with an eye on the trades unions, cut back the immigrant intake, although considerable numbers are still admitted to join the work force, and to take the place of those who have left the country for other parts of the world.

At its meeting in August 1972, the General Council of the Library Association of Australia had before it a submission that there were significant groups in the Australian community which were being deprived, possibly by default, of library services suitable to their needs, but to which they were entitled as citizens. These groups included immigrants, Australian aborigines, and people in isolated rural communities. Council agreed substantially with the submission but considered that a closer examination of the problems involved was required before initiating any action. Accordingly, it authorised a pilot survey to be made of special library services available to immigrants in New South Wales.(1)

The terms of reference for the survey required that investigations should be made on two fronts: first, a determination, through consultation of relevant statistics, of the number of adults and children involved, divided by nationality and age-group and resident in the various local government areas in the state; and, second, an enquiry into the local library situation that would indicate the existence of any services designed specifically for immigrants and provided on a federal, state or local government level, or indeed by association or agency, governmental or otherwise.

The terms of reference did not envisage any direct contact with immigrants, either individually or in groups, in order to ascertain their views on special library services, although obviously it was expected that the findings of the survey would indicate avenues for consultation and cooperation. Recommendations were not called for on any follow-up action deemed to be necessary. In the event, the compiler of the report did draw conclusions from the exercise and did make some basic suggestions for a general improvement in the extremely limited library services provided for immigrants in New South Wales. It was also assumed that, always allowing for differences in the sizes of the immigrant populations, the operation of state library services, and in local attitudes, the situation in the other five states would be substantially the same as that in New South Wales. It was confidently expected that there would be strong similarities between the two most populous states, New South Wales and Victoria, which housed the important manufacturing complexes and, therefore, employed the greatest numbers of immigrant workers, English-speaking and otherwise.

In conducting the survey, coverage where practicable was given to the role of libraries in the provision of special materials for those learning English as a second language, to cooperation between librarians and educators, and to the availability in libraries of foreign language books, magazines, newspapers and other materials which could enable the newcomers and their children to retain contact with their own cultural heritage.

Operation of the survey revealed some interesting statistical data on the immigrant population of Australia, even though the full details of the 1971 census were not then available(2) and figures from the 1966 census were the only guide to immigrant population by nationality and age group. Problems which presented themselves included the fact that the 1971 figures were already out of date owing to immigrant mobility, and to arrivals and departures since the census was taken. Another unknown factor was the number of immigrants who might have avoided inclusion in the census. Moreover, although the figures revealed the numbers of people born outside Australia and their country of origin, they did not reveal such things as length of residence in Australia, degree of literacy in their own language, ability to speak English on arrival, standard of education or, not surprisingly, the degree of access to books and libraries in their mother countries. Another problem resulted from a rather unfortunate tendency to group diverse nationalities under such headings as 'other European', 'Asian, and so on, which prevented among other things, the compilation of figures for Spanish, Turkish, Lebanese and French immigrants.

It was decided to ignore statistics of immigrants from English-speaking countries except in so far as they contributed to area totals. This was done on the assumption that most migrants from Canada, New Zealand, Eire, the United States and the United Kingdom would already be familiar with public and other library services and, on arrival in New South Wales, would only require to be put in touch with the nearest appropriate library to their residence or place of work. It certainly could not be ignored that by far the largest number of immigrants were shown to be from English-speaking countries. Thus in 1971 there were in the state, 79,974 Italians (the largest non-English group) as against 262,918 persons from England alone.

The 1966 census figures(3) were so out-of-date that it was felt that only very general assumptions could be drawn from them, and in the event they tended to reinforce what was already common knowledge. The bulk of immigrants of whatever nationality were within age groups ranging from twenty to fifty nine years. There were fewer older people, although obviously this grouping would increase proportionately as time passed. There were large families of children, particularly in the case of the Greeks and Italians, and in many cases more men than women, for example among the Yugoslavs, Greeks and Italians. This is a difficult social problem. Moreover, the figures showed that migrants tend to congregate in urban areas, for of the 8,710 Greek males in 1966 aged between thirty and thirty nine years, no less than 7,458 were living in the Sydney metropolitan area. Again the large numbers of children shown in urban metropolitan statistics suggested problems in the field of education as a whole and not merely in library service. In 1966, there were about 10,000 Italians under the age of nineteen, 2,300 Yugoslavs (these numbers would have risen sharply since then), 5,500 Maltese, 6,300 Greeks and 2,000 Egyptians all of school age or under and living in metropolitan areas.

What did the 1971 census reveal? First, that there was a wide spread of nationalities in every local government area in the state. Second, that immigrants were mainly congregated in the Sydney metropolitan area, in the cities of Newcastle and Greater Wollongong, with comparatively small numbers in country towns and outlying rural localities. Third, even in Sydney, large concentrations of immigrants were only to be found in a limited number of suburbs, sometimes with one nationality predominant, sometimes with several groups, as in the suburbs of Blacktown,

Fairfield and Marrickville. This tendency to group together was perhaps related to availability of employment, perhaps to the influence of a church and its pastors (for example, the Greek Orthodox Church at Marrickville), or to a search for self protection and community of interest and language with fellow nationals.

In almost every area the largest immigrant component was of English-speaking origin, and this group dominated the numbers of those shown to have been born outside Australia. Nevertheless, in a few local government areas in Sydney, and in Greater Wollongong (home of the iron and steel industry) there were unusually large concentrations of English-speaking immigrants. Hence, the inner city municipality of Marrickville, after excluding immigrants of English-speaking origin, had a population of whom 35% were born outside Australia - mainly Greeks, Yugoslavs and Turks. Other municipalities had concentrations of 20% or more but in a few areas, the numbers were relatively insignificant. Factors which the statistics did not reveal included length of residence in Australia, degree of integration into the local society, and ability to communicate in, or fluency in, English.

Taking the five years prior to 1973, a striking feature was the rapid build-up of a few nationalities in certain urban areas. This was the outcome of governmental recruitment policies, political and economic problems in particular countries, and a tendency on the part of immigrants to group with persons of their own nationality or where work is more readily available. Immigrants from Greece, Yugoslavia, Turkey and South America, particularly Chile, came in increasing numbers. Between 1967 and 1971, Wollongong had an increase in its migrant population of 14,094, of whom almost 4,000 were Yugoslavs with little or no fluency in English and, on the whole, of a relatively low standard of education. Looking at New South Wales as a whole there were in 1971, 51,758 Yugoslavs as against 27,400 in 1966. Turkish arrivals increased by over 500% during the same period. The total population of New South Wales in 1971 was 4,579,932 of whom 871,767 were born outside Australia, either in English speaking countries or elsewhere - a proportion of one in five.

The official attitude of the library service to non English-speaking immigrants was, and is, that they should learn at least the rudiments of English as soon as possible after their arrival. There is a certain amount of common sense in this as the newcomers have to live, eat, work and travel in a community which to an overwhelming degree has no expertise in any language but English, and shows no desire to become either bilingual or multilingual. Employers expect their factory hands and workmen to learn the job mostly from directions given only in English. And so on. Unfortunately, very little attention has been paid to the standards of literacy reached by immigrants in their own country and, at best, only a patchy effort has been made to assist newcomers culturally and socially as members of their new community.

It is quite obvious that immigrants as members of the general public are entitled to the same library services as Australian-born citizens. However, their capacity to take advantage of these services may be prevented or inhibited by a number of factors which include:- inability to speak, or lack of fluency in English; ignorance of the whereabouts of public and other libraries and their rights to membership: shyness in a new land and a strange environment; concentration on getting homes and jobs and generally 'settling in'; a low standard of literacy in their old country and a poor standard of education; lack of interest in books and reading; lack of suitable material, particularly for those seeking to improve their command of English; a dearth of books, magazines and newspapers in foreign languages; lack of language expertise among librarians; and lack of contact between librarians and immigrants through the medium of say, hostels, clubs, churches and ethnic and social groups.

What might immigrants require from libraries? The needs of both adults and children may be said to fall into four categories: material to assist them to learn English as a second language, for instance audio-visual software, books, magazines and so on; information about Australia and Australians, with emphasis on factual information dealing with government and government services, social welfare, local rules and regulations, customs of the country, indigenous flora and fauna and similar information; material to enable them to maintain contact with their own culture and homeland, including such items of a purely recreational nature as fiction, newspapers, popular illustrated magazines, and, where possible, tapes, discs, films and prints; specially selected material in English with a relatively simple vocabulary to help immigrant students of all ages, since the language of the ordinary textbooks may be too complex for ready assimilation.

Assuming, hopefully, that all library services in New South Wales were available to as many of the newcomers as were willing and able to take advantage of them, attention was directed to special services provided for immigrant users.(4) These could emanate from various sources: local government, the Australian Department of Immigration, either acting on its own or through the State Education Department, migrant clubs and welfare associations, the State Library of New South Wales, or indeed, any other library or organisation interested in migrant education, welfare or social integration. No special investigation was directed towards library services in tertiary institutions, as it was assumed that those accepted as students had already acquired sufficient expertise in English to enable them to study, and that individuals in need of help would receive sympathetic attention from librarians engaged in reader education in those institutions.

Relevant contacts were made wherever possible to seek out the information desired and, in addition, a questionnaire was distributed to sixty two local government library services in New South Wales. This questionnaire evoked a ninety three percent response. The questionnaire sought to obtain information within five main headings:-

1   To establish whether librarians were aware of significant groups of immigrants living within their service areas, and of the predominant nationalities.

2   To find out whether immigrants were using the library service and what, if anything, librarians did to encourage membership, including the provision of any special facilities.

3   To learn what books were in the libraries in languages other than English.

4   To find out what cooperation or liaison existed between local libraries and other bodies concerned in any way with the social, educational and cultural needs of immigrants.

5   To enquire what librarians considered future policies should be, in particular regarding the provision of materials in foreign languages in order to enable immigrants and their children to maintain contact with their own cultural heritage, and also to help widen Australian horizons.

The questionnaire provided some interesting reading. All librarians were aware of the presence of immigrants within their service areas, but only half of those interviewed found the numbers to be really significant and these were located in urban areas. Only five mentioned the British immigrants as a significant grouping although in almost every local government area they are by far the most numerous. It was apparent that the word 'immigrant' to many must have meant non English-speaking or 'foreign'. Most reported that they felt immigrants wanted books in their own languages, books to help them learn English, fiction in English, and books about Australia its life and customs.

A depressingly small number of librarians reported any effort to encourage immigrants to use libraries. However, in about ten areas where there were really large numbers of newcomers of various nationalities, some positive steps have been taken. Very few libraries, however, have had any contact with immigrant clubs or associations, and cooperation between libraries and the representatives of immigrants appeared to be virtually non-existent. Nevertheless, some contact with schools containing a large immigrant element was reported.

Only about half of the libraries surveyed reported that they had any foreign language books, and in most cases the holdings were quite negligible. In fact the total holdings for the state were quite ludicrous considering the numbers of immigrants involved. Thus in a statewide bookstock of 20,028 volumes some twenty five languages were covered, and in only seven languages did the stock come to more than 1,000 books. An example of the futility of these holdings can be taken from the provision of books in the Italian and Greek languages. There were 1,894 Italian books as against the 79,974 Italians living in the state. The figures for Greek books were even worse, with 347 volumes for 53,039 people.

Librarians claimed to make as much use as possible of the inter-library loan machinery in order to eke out local book stocks and assist their readers. Enquiries were usually directed to the extension service of the Library of New South Wales, and to the metropolitan public libraries which were members of the Sydney Subject Specialisation Scheme. Many reported difficulty in obtaining suitable foreign language material, especially books for children and recreational materials. So far as the future was concerned, librarians interviewed favoured increasing their own foreign language holdings, given adequate finance, available suppliers, and sufficient multi-lingual members of staff to select and acquire suitable materials, and to make proper contact with immigrant users of the library. There was strong support for the idea of establishing a centrally organised pool of books in at least the most common languages. Material from this pool would then be available for consultation on the spot or sent out either on interlibrary loan or on bulk loan.

Apart from such facilities as existed within the local public library service, special library services for immigrants were virtually non-existent in New South Wales. At government level there appeared to be neither special services nor a stated policy on the subject. Thus the Australian Department of Immigration, the Australian and New South Wales Department of Education, the State Department of Technical Education, the Institute of Languages at the University of New South Wales, the Library of New South Wales and the State School Library Service all proved wanting in this direction. Such services to immigrants as had been provided by some of these departments and institutions had been mainly in the field of teaching English as a second language. School library facilities available to immigrant children tended to be good, bad or indifferent according to the area where the school was located, the excellence or otherwise of the library, and the enthusiasm and dedication of individual teachers and librarians.

Consideration of the available statistics, replies to the questionnaire, and information gleaned from personal contact and enquiry led one to the following conclusions:

1 There appeared to have been no objective study of the immigrant community to establish its social needs, needs of which library service was but one facet.

2 There was in the state no coherent policy on library services to immigrants, nor indeed, any understanding of their needs in this area.

3 Special, as opposed to ordinary, library services could be described as almost non-existent, and such services as were provided resulted more from the efforts of devoted individuals then from any official policy.

4 Very little effort was being made to inform new immigrants, English-speaking or otherwise, of the existence and location of public and other libraries and of their rights thereto as members of the community.

5 There was, to an alarming extent, lack of liaison between

169

persons and bodies associated with immigrants (for instance, relevant government departments, teachers, librarians, social and community workers, and the immigrants' own cultural and welfare organisations.

6   The provision of foreign language collections in the state was quite inadequate to meet the cultural and recreational needs of immigrants.

7   There were insufficient librarians possessed of the necessary language qualifications either to work with immigrant users or to handle foreign language materials of all kinds.

8   There was a lack of simple adult material to enable immigrants to gain greater fluency in English, and to bridge the gap between the structured readers used in education classes and ordinary books of fiction or information which demand too much of learners of English.

9   That it was not easy to find reliable local suppliers of foreign language books, magazines and other materials in many of the tongues spoken by immigrants. Regrettably, childrens' books familiar to immigrants in their mother tongue were extremely difficult to obtain.

It would be pleasant but misleading to report that great strides have been made since 1973, but at least some tentative steps have been taken, not only in the field of special library services to immigrants but also in community attitudes and involvement. Another pleasing development has been a more vocal participation by the new-comers themselves to secure greater recognition of their needs and to make known their own point of view. Nowhere has there been more progress than in the field of education where, at last, a more intelligent approach has been taken towards the teaching of English as a second language to adults and children. Another advance has been in the appointment of special teachers to help in schools where there are numbers of children with language difficulties.

Although the Australian Government has cut back the immigration quotas, many new settlers are still coming in and there does seem to be more offical interest in their wellbeing after arrival. However, the Department of Immigration has been dismembered and its functions spread over three other departments. Not unnaturally, this has prevented the making of rapid progress. Despite the efforts of the Library Association of

Australia(5) to convince the Australian Government of the need for a more positive approach to information and library services for immigrants, no real breakthrough can be reported, and no overall fund allocations have been made. School libraries in general have received very substantial injections of Government funds, therefore the children of immigrants will benefit from the improved facilities, the audio-visual equipment and the increased bookstocks thus provided. They will even more certainly benefit from the specialised instruction in English from teachers seconded to school staffs for the purpose.

It is still true to say that there is no coordinated policy on library and information services to immigrants but increasing numbers of librarians in all types if libraries are showing more awareness of the problems involved, and are contributing so far as they are able with their limited financial resources by making improvements in their own services and awakening interest and cooperation amongst immigrant groups and the general public. Attempts to provide library service to immigrants will face similar problems in all the Australian states and a brief look at some of the activities now going on in the states of New South Wales and Victoria could serve as a guide to some potentially useful avenues of approach. The State Library of New South Wales is engaged in a pilot project to set up a centralised pool of foreign language books to be administered through its extension service. Some 20,000 dollars has been set aside during the current financial year for the purchase of books for this purpose, and should the pilot scheme prove successful, further action and development will follow.

At Bankstown Municipality in Sydney, the public library has always played a prominent part in community service and involvement. Its ongoing interest is to make the library a meeting place and a centre for community integration. The library has a committee with immigrant participation and it is engaged in a programme called 'Passport to the World', where immigrants can be involved in demonstrating the culture and customs of their homelands. The library guide has inserts in a variety of languages, and immigrants have helped in translating a precis of the guide into their own languages. The librarian hopes to make the library a multi-cultural centre, not just a meeting place for separate ethnic groups.

171

Marrickville Municipality has likewise been active in community work with immigrants. The librarians there have been closely involved in local projects, latterly with the Community Advice Committee which operates under the Australian Assistance Plan. The library has received 10,000 dollars as part of a grant from the Australian Grants Commission to the Council, for the purchase of foreign language books and audio-visual material. The library is helped in the acquisition and cataloguing of this material by two Egyptian and one Greek members of staff. The latter imports books and records for the library.

Blacktown is another rapidly growing municipality located in the western suburbs or Sydney where there are a great many community problems. The library staff is active in building up goodwill amongst the immigrant community and has set up a committee of representatives of ethnic groups and the library staff with the aim of creating a two-way exchange of ideas and pooling experience. The library received from the Department of Urban and Regional Development a grant to set up a language laboratory and to purchase the necessary software. This enterprise is operating at present in a limited way, mainly owing to the difficulties of obtaining tapes and records suitable for the language needs of the Blacktown community.

The Department of Urban and Regional Development has also allocated 94,000 dollars to the Library Council of Victoria for the purchase. of foreign language books for the western region — an experimental planning region which the Australian Government is using as a proving ground for future regional development. Amongst Victorian libraries, Coburg, with Italians and Yugoslavs being the two dominant immigrant groups, has built up a reasonable collection of foreign language books for both adults and children. It also operates a small programme of storytelling in Greek, Turkish and Italian. At Sunshine, there are over 4,000 foreign language books and a representative collection of journals in over twelve languages. There are also folk music records in Italian, Greek and Serbo-Croatian. Publicity material is prepared in multi-lingual form. A high proportion of the staff is European born and can assist newcomers. Members of the immigrant community can also prove helpful when translation services are required. To facilitate such developments the library liaises with ethnic and national groups.

The Moomee Valley Regional Library serves a total population of 220,000 on the outskirts of Melbourne. There are many immigrants in the area, including over 22,000 Italians and more than 8,000 Greeks. The library service is very active in community involvement. In 1974 so far as immigrants were concerned, English language classes for housewives were begun, an Italian children's party was organised to launch the Junior Italian Collection, Greek and Italian nights were held, and purchases were made of Italian children's books and of Greek, Turkish and Yugoslav titles.

The St Kilda Library in an inner suburb of Melbourne has a varied collection of foreign language books. It intends to give more attention to the provision of recreational reading matter in the future. More adult books than children's ones are borrowed from the library, and newspapers and periodicals are in popular demand. A community noticeboard displays all materials available on local services for immigrants, and the pamphlet file has all that can be assembled about Australian and Victorian Government sources of assistance. This latter facility is extremely popular. Many adult immigrants join the library after their children have paid class visits to it, particularly where the family structure is still strong. The librarian, Mrs Vida Horn and Miss Margaret Dunkle have received a grant from the Library Council of Victoria for a project on the preparation of children's picture books with parallel texts in selected foreign languages.

The city of Williamstown has a population of 30,000, of which ten percent is non English-speaking. The local library will receive part of the 94,000 dollars granted for the Western Region Foreign Language Collection, and will include paperbacks and popular magazines in the collection. Acquisition will at first be concentrated on books in the major languages, Greek, Italian and Yugoslav, but over thirty languages are represented in the area. A literacy programme for immigrants based on the library is now at the planning stage.

The last service to be mentioned is the important Geelong Regional Library, which through nine libraries and three bookmobiles serves the state's second city, and covers both industrial and rural areas. In 1974, the library made two surveys of loans of foreign language books correlated with the current bookstock and numbers of immigrant users. These provided the information necessary to build a better balanced collection. The Dutch are the most enthusiastic group of foreign language readers in Geelong, although their command of English is good. There is a need for many more Italian books however. An experiment in printing membership application cards in six languages is now underway, and displays have been arranged at Migrant Information Services in two city banks. In 1974 also, the library appointed an agent to buy Polish books while he was visiting his homeland. This idea proved to be so successful that the experiment has been repeated with German books. Staff members have skills in eleven languages and this has helped in building up community contacts.

There is obviously still much to be done in the field of library service to immigrants in Australia but a start has been made. More interaction is going to be needed with the immigrant community in order to establish real cultural and informational needs. One plain fact which cannot be emphasised too often is that no substantial improvement in the lot of the immigrant in Australia will be made until all branches of government and officialdom take a genuine interest in the problems involved, and make available adequate facilities and finance to those persons and groups in the community, both Australian and immigrant, who can work together for the common good. In any endeavours in the future, librarians would be expected to play their part by offering high standards of service to every member of the multi-racial community. To quote from Jefferson's *Libraries and society* (6) 'Any discrimination on the grounds of race, religion or colour is anathema to the library service. Library provision is guided by the ideal that it is a social institution of a kind that can, by appropriate bookstock and extension activities, help to reduce the difficulties of assimilation confronting a racial minority yet provide for the native literature needs of ethnic groups'. This should be the aim of Australian library service to immigrants.

REFERENCES

1 Library Association of Australia *General council meeting 1972, minute 77/72.*

2 Australia. Bureau of Census and Statistics *Census of population and housing 1971.*

3 Australia. Bureau of Census and Statistics *Census of*

population and housing 1966.

4 Library Association of Australia *Pilot survey of special library services available to migrants in New South Wales* 1973.

5 Library Association of Australia *Library services of migrants — submission to Migrant Task Force Committee, New South Wales* 1973.

6 G Jefferson *Library and society* London, James Clarke and Co, 1969.

DEVELOPED AND DEVELOPING COUNTRIES, AN EVOLUTIONARY PROCESS?

KEN GILMORE

Senior Lecturer, Department of Library and Information Service. Tasmanian College of Advanced Education

Disadvantaged, is a term used frequently throughout the world today by an ever increasing number of people. The term means many things to many people. A study of English language dictionaries reveals a common approach: all have something to say about prejudice, absence or lack of advantage, or unfavourable circumstances, but very few attempt to qualify this. Perhaps the best definition is to be found in Websters *New collegiate dictionary* (Springfield, Mass, Merriam, 1973) where disadvantaged is defined as 'lacking in the basic resources or conditions (as standard housing, medical and educational facilities and civil rights) believed to be necessary for an equal position in society'. A question that this definition immediately poses is, can there ever be anyone who is advantaged? Perhaps somewhere there is someone! Rather an extreme approach but one which it is logical to consider. The vogue in the use of the term, disadvantaged, has been brought about as some governments have initiated programmes in an attempt to remove some of this disadvantage and to make society more equal, and as action groups become more concerned with their fellow human being and their problems. Migrants, the physically handicapped, the poor, the economically blighted, the sick, the aged, are just a few of the groups in society to whom the term disadvantaged has been applied.

What is the relevance of all this to library service? Most relevant is the service provided by the public library which is the type of library most involved in service to the disadvantaged. Should the public library be making a fuss about special services to these groups of people? They do, and one can read the never-ending saga of library programmes to the sick, the poor, the migrant and so on in the professional literature, and one's heart is touched by the good done.

The public library is basically a middle class institution in a community where reading is considered desirable, and as such when service is given outside this elitist group, we find a great deal of fuss about bringing attention to the service. Perhaps this may be justified as advertising to attract the potential group or groups to be served, but certainly not as an attempt to measure the amount of potential good which might be done by some do-gooder librarian. If the public library has the right outlook, it should automatically offer its services to the entire community. As such it should act as the community's information centre; a place at which any individual can obtain the information be it technical, educational, social or financial. How many public libraries actually operate in this manner? Very few, as this approach to the role of the public library in a community is not seen by administrators and this information role is usurped by government departments, commercial agencies such as building information centres, or volunteer groups such as citizens advice bureaux. Perhaps this growth in public information outlets has come about as the public library has failed to adjust to changes in society.

With the diversity of information outlets what is the public library left with? A collection of books for those people who can read; and it is generally known that the level of illiteracy through-out the world is high. Even in 'developed' countries of the industrialised world such as Australia, many children leave school without having acquired the necessary skills to read, and many leave with a minimal level of reading skills which will deteriorate without constant reinforcement. To them, and a large percentage of those who can read, the public library is irrelevant as a collection of books.

The public library with its narrow book-orientated outlook housed in some inadequate location is all too often the traditional image held by most people. Certainly this is the truth in many communities, and because of this, the library cannot be a dynamic force. In some communities, the public library occupies its rightful place as a dynamic force and this, of course, should be the aim of all concerned with public library work. The range of materials available often helps determine this, as one finds collections of gramophone records, tape cassettes, films, posters, art prints, sets of plays, music, original art by local artists, and objects such as woodcarvings and pottery, all available for loan. Not only an extended range of material helps, but also giving total library service and acting as a community information centre where any individual can gain access to information on any subject at any depth in any form, whether this individual or group of individuals fall into the disadvantaged category or the advantaged category. Few public libraries operate at this level. This is because the attitudes of librarians, the holders of the purse strings, or the individuals in the community; each or all may be unsympathetic. Ignorance, illiteracy, laziness, apathy, hostility are just a few of the words which apply in this case.

Librarians must be continually assessing their work, and must change along with changes in society. Some people would see the public library as having a responsibility to social change and evolution by helping people gain access to information on topics of current or future interest, and which is hard to obtain. As such they need to be well ahead of the changes in society in their awareness and planning. How many librarians are currently planning for, or have even given a thought to library services in 1984 or 2001? If not, why not is the next question. Conservatism, laziness, or lack of professionalism may be some of the points to be considered. Frequently librarians have become overconcerned with the technical aspects of librarianship, and as such forget why their library is there, even perhaps becoming oblivious to the fact that their library is for people. This attitude is found throughout the world, and it comes as a breath of fresh air, when one comes across a dynamic library actively involved with its community. As such it will serve the disadvantaged groups as a matter of course, and will not give itself a pat on the back for doing good.

Finance may limit the development of effective library service, but the lack of finance is often a reflection on the inadequacy of the librarian. This situation is largely due to the ineffectiveness of the librarians in making sure that the library service receives its proper share of the available finance. Administrators in local government often have a strange idea of what the role of a library is, and unfortunately, the idea of a library as a collection of books ranks high on the list. Few see the public library as capable of providing an information service as outlined above, and consequently, the librarian has a real problem to change these old fashioned ideas and concepts. Attitude change is hard and challenging work, so few librarians accept the challenge to enlighten the administrators of the need for change or of the library's proper role, and subsequently, sink further back into oblivion and irrelevance to their community with their collecion of books. One of the concerns of the administrators is in financial accountability, and they see it difficult to measure what they get out of the library service for the financial input. Although hard to measure, and expensive, a good service is essential to modern society. What is important is that libraries relate to current trends, and currently throughout the world governments are paying a great deal of attention to man and his recreation. How many public libraries are using this bandwagon to advance their library and its service? Not too many!

As one examines the people who work in libraries as so-called professional librarians, it becomes apparent that many lack professionalism. This group is one of the biggest millstones around the neck of library development, whether they be in a developing country or in a 'developed' country. The acquisition of a library qualification from a library school does not automatically make one a professional librarian; the right attitude of mind has to be there, and to this extent, library schools have a huge responsibility in the selection of the right people and in profes-sional attitude formulation. With this, the task of bringing about change will be easier, but still an uphill battle as the profession will always be lumbered with this lethargic and pathetic millstone in some form or another.

Change is also necessary in the attitudes of the individuals in the community. To the majority of them, the public library is a totally irrelevant institution. To many, the library as a community institution is a nonentity as they have never experienced library service, either at school, at work or in their community, and are most unlikely ever to do so in the remainder of their lifetime. One of the reasons is that their public library in its present form is virtually incapable of giving a relevant service to its community! Another is that libraries do little to advertise their services in an attempt to advise the community just what the library has to offer. This is understandable as a sudden increase in the demand for service would be an embarassment, as most public libraries are not geared to give service to their entire community. Most relate to their community as a lender of books to a percentage of the community. Has anyone thought of knocking on household

179

doors and telling people about the public library? Librarians are so concerned with library routines that they will meticulously file main entries, create added entries and worry about classification· tables, and then claim to have no time for work in the community.

The need for change is supreme, but it is slow, and owing to this slowness, gradually in many communities the public library becomes more irrelevant. In this context, attempts at service to the disadvantaged may be singled out for attention, and lumps of goodness measured. On the other end of the spectrum, many libraries are actively involved in programmes in which they are working with these so-called disadvantaged, and as such have a contribution to make. Just as there are problems in the school library serving the school community, or the special library serving its community, then there are problems and philosophies to be discussed and resolved when the public library attempts to serve the disadvantaged groups as part of its total service. As such the professional literature is justified in devoting space to library service to the disadvantaged.

Is there an evolutionary pattern which can be traced in the development of library service to the disadvantaged? Is there any comparison which can be made between the developing countries of the third world and the developed areas of the world? It is hard to generalise on either count, and though personal observation helps, it would not give the remainder of the article a scientific base. Perhaps this does not matter; the important thing being that all communities, irrespective of whether they are advantaged or disadvantaged, have access to effective total library service.

Developing countries comprise a large portion of the world, and are all at various levels in their development process, as they attempt to emulate the developed countries. Many do not like the stigma of the term 'developing', and prefer to be known as an emerging nation, or as part of the third world bloc. Irrespective of the terminology, writers in the field of development theory generally agree that there is a common evolutionary pattern. T Dos Santos(1) summarizes this in the following terms;

1 Development means advancement towards certain well defined general objectives which correspond to the specific conditions of man and society to be found in the most

advanced societies of the modern world. The model is variously known as modern society, industrial society, mass society and so on.

2 Underdeveloped countries will progress towards this model as they have eliminated certain social, political, cultural and institutional obstacles. These obstacles are represented by 'traditional societies', 'feudal systems' or 'feudal residues', depending on the particular school of thought.

3 Certain economic, political and psychological processes can be singled out as allowing the most rational mobilization of national resources, and these can be categorised for the use of economic planners.

4 To all this is added the need to coordinate certain social and political forces in support of a development policy and to devise an ideological basis which organises the will of various nations in the 'tasks' of development.

Given that a developing society attempts to develop along the lines of the most advanced societies of the modern world, then libraries must be relevant. Their relevance may be questioned, and their level of operation varies greatly. Somehow, the library does not have a very large role to play in a developing country, at least, not the public library. Other types of library, for example, university, national and special, have more relevance, but only to a very small percentage of the educated people.

Library development in developing nations does follow the same basic evolutionary pattern, This can be observed from a study of library development in the countries of Asia, Africa and South America. In this pattern, public library service and school library service are virtually non-existent. As such, there can be no attempt at library service to disadvantaged groups. Libraries in a developing country are just as elitist, if not even more so, than in a developed country. Basically, this is due to the fact that a large percentage of the population is illiterate, and will remain that way for the rest of their lives. Even though there may be compulsory primary school education, it does little to help alleviate the illiteracy problem. Furthermore, with no public libraries worthy of mention, no change can be expected. A further reason relates to the availability of finance. Obviously within any planned development programme, there is limited finance, and somehow in the allocation of funds, the administrators see that dams, running water, health programmes, factories, government office blocks are high on the priority list. They fail to understand that a public library has a definite role to play as they attempt to remove the earlier mentioned obstacles.

Libraries in a developing country are not overlooked. One usually finds a national library of a kind: this is usually one of the many national institutions, for example, national museum, national art gallery, which spring up along with government attempts to evolve a national spirit. The national library is usually housed in either temporary or unsatisfactory accomodation or in a rather splendid architectural structure: the library will have acute shortage of funds, be poorly staffed, have a poor collection except with its own national material, and will be attempting to give a national bibliographic service. Basically, it will be a national library in name only. A number of special libraries will operate very efficiently and successfully. This section will be covering a very special information field and serving a closely-knit community. As such it is easy for them to operate, as they are usually a key part in the government's development programme. They are found within the national airline system, the national radio and television service, the national bank, some government departments, such as defence, and in specialised research institutes, usually in relation to agriculture and to those products upon which the country's economy is dependant. An example of this is the library at the Malaysian Rubber Research Institute, which has a large collection of highly specialised material in the field of rubber. Libraries relating to medicine and dentistry will usually occur, being located within medical or dental schools, or at the large central hospital. All the fore-going special libraries are an integral part of the development process, and as such are well-financed and well-staffed.

The institutes of higher learning are usually well favoured with regard to libraries. They are seen as a status symbol in the country's development, and as they tend to follow a western model. a large centralised library is part of the institution. Usually, the library will be housed in a modern architectural structure looking just like those seen in North America, Australia, or Western Europe. The collections will reflect the institution's teaching programme, be largely in English, and serve partly as a textbook service as many titles will be duplicated by up to twenty copies.

Reader service will be almost non-existent, except for a rigidly controlled loan service; few students knowing that they might even ask a librarian for help. The library will also act as a study hall where students produce essays and assignments, as the university library offers a more pleasant environment than the usual sub-standard student accomodation. The librarians will be concerned with collection development, attempting to develop a national research collection of sorts, and they will compete with other institutions in the country to be the biggest and the best. As such these libraries are, and do virtually nothing to help the student, whether advantaged or disadvantaged.

The public library occupies a very low key position amongst all this; that is, if it exists at all. Perhaps what is called a public library is really a subscription library lending books for a fee to those who can read. Maybe it is a free public library, but does little more than lend books; the reason being perfectly clear, a basic lack of money. As such no one has a 'hear a book' programme, worries about picture books for the ghetto children, goes on ward rounds to hospital patients, or takes a book-mobile service to the prison. Neither is there any service to business and industry, any tape cassettes, prints for loan, and all those things and activities one expects to find in a public library in a developed country. When do they ever start to give total community library service? Perhaps in 2001, but certainly not in the early stages of development. Those whom are considered 'disadvantaged' in a developed country are virtually ignored on all fronts in a developing society. One has only to see the masses of beggers and children suffering from malnutrition, and the poor living conditions of the working class in most of the developing countries. In contrast one can see the opulence of the rich side by side: to all the public library is irrelevant. Librarians in such countries have to look very deeply into the crystal ball if they are even to think about library service to the disadvantaged in a realistic way.

What about the developed countries? Is there an evolutionary pattern? It is very hard to generalise on a world-wide basis, and articles elsewhere in this volume illustrate some of the work being done. Why do these programmes come about? Many reasons including government funds and their availability, a re-examination of some of the values of society, a growing concern for people, a realisation of the potential of the public library, and the trendiness which prompts some librarians to hop on the band-wagon and hope to make a name for themselves by pretending to work with the so-called disadvantaged. It is not too hard to think of someone who fits into this latter category.

In many of the developed countries, governments have become very concerned with the problems of minorities, perhaps ethnic, sexual, economic, and as such large sums of government money raised through taxation are spent on programmes to remove the disadvantaged position of these groups. Examples of this are the large sums of money spent in the United States in the 1960s and the early 1970s, and the money which is currently being made available under the Australian Assistance Plan. Some of this money goes to public libraries which permits the development of collections and services relevant to the community served. Perhaps a key factor in the development of library service to the disadvantaged is the government's ability to raise funds to finance such programmes. Does this occur during boom times, and then when the need comes to contract in lean times, do such services contract or disappear altogether? Is the word 'disadvantaged' a bandwagon which governments grasp at as society undergoes a certain change?

Life styles have undergone a great change in developed countries here, but our advances in science and technology have allowed us to prolong human life, thus a larger percentage of population fits into the category, 'aged', and that group is considered disadvantaged. Zero population growth, real concern for conservation and environment, drugs, a freer attitude to sexuality, shorter working hours and more leisure time, and concern for the third world are just some of the features of the modern developed country. So too, is a deep interest in the word 'community'. Does the developed society look back to the remnants of the preliterate society currently becoming a developing society for the true meaning of this word? Libraries did not exist in pre-literate society, but these societies functioned perfectly well and still do so without a public library. Is the library really an irrelevant institution which is slowly dying a natural death? Perhaps so, unless it relates to the aged, the problems of having increased time for recreation, and other changes in life style. Changes take place gradually, and one which is becoming more apparent is the concern with the individual and with self-expression. Part of this change is manifested in the public library realising it has to relate to a community. This realisation comes slowly to most librarians and therefore the public library is a relevant institution in only a very few communities. Other agencies usurp the activities of an aware public library, for example, the libraries found in migrant clubs in Australia. Where the public librarian is fully aware of the nature of his or her community, total community library service will be given, and the aged will be served with large print books, the migrant will have his books in his own language, the foundry can have help in its managerial problem, the deserted wife can find out where to turn to for social welfare and so on.

All that is needed to achieve this is a blank cheque, a more open attitude by more librarians to giving total community library service, and a curbing of existing tendencies to hop on any bandwagon. That evolutionary process: does it exist? Perhaps only in the availability of the finance to give the services we all know are needed, and dream of as an ideal. Why it is some library services come close to achieving the ideal and other fail dismally? The apathy of their librarians. As a librarian, you, the reader are responsible for the future of library services to the disadvantaged section of society. When you have accepted this responsibility and begin to orient your library system towards community involvement, then, and only then, can you call yourself a librarian.

REFERENCES

1   T Dos Santos 'The crisis in development theory and the problem of dependence in Latin America' In, *Underdevelopment and development, the third world today; selected readings,* edited by Henry Bernstein, Penguin, 1973. 58-59.